WITHDRAWN

The New
Gold Standard

The New Gold Standard

WITHDRAWN

Rediscovering the Power of Gold to Protect and Grow Wealth

Paul Nathan

WILEY

John Wiley & Sons, Inc.

Lincoln Public Library   DUPL

3 7496 00328551 4

Copyright © 2011 by Paul Nathan. All rights reserved.

Published by John Wiley & Sons, Inc., Hoboken, New Jersey.
Published simultaneously in Canada.

No part of this publication may be reproduced, stored in a retrieval system, or transmitted in any form or by any means, electronic, mechanical, photocopying, recording, scanning, or otherwise, except as permitted under Section 107 or 108 of the 1976 United States Copyright Act, without either the prior written permission of the Publisher, or authorization through payment of the appropriate per-copy fee to the Copyright Clearance Center, Inc., 222 Rosewood Drive, Danvers, MA 01923, (978) 750-8400, fax (978) 646-8600, or on the Web at www.copyright.com. Requests to the Publisher for permission should be addressed to the Permissions Department, John Wiley & Sons, Inc., 111 River Street, Hoboken, NJ 07030, (201) 748-6011, fax (201) 748-6008, or online at http://www.wiley.com/go/permissions.

Limit of Liability/Disclaimer of Warranty: While the publisher and author have used their best efforts in preparing this book, they make no representations or warranties with respect to the accuracy or completeness of the contents of this book and specifically disclaim any implied warranties of merchantability or fitness for a particular purpose. No warranty may be created or extended by sales representatives or written sales materials. The advice and strategies contained herein may not be suitable for your situation. You should consult with a professional where appropriate. Neither the publisher nor author shall be liable for any loss of profit or any other commercial damages, including but not limited to special, incidental, consequential, or other damages.

For general information on our other products and services or for technical support, please contact our Customer Care Department within the United States at (800) 762-2974, outside the United States at (317) 572-3993 or fax (317) 572-4002.

Designations used by companies to distinguish their products are often claimed by trademarks. In all instances where the author or publisher is aware of a claim, the product names appear in Initial Capital letters. Readers, however, should contact the appropriate companies for more complete information regarding trademarks and registration.

Wiley also publishes its books in a variety of electronic formats. Some content that appears in print may not be available in electronic formats. For more information about Wiley products, visit our web site at www.wiley.com.

Library of Congress Cataloging-in-Publication Data:

Nathan, Paul, 1944–
    The new gold standard : rediscovering the power of gold to protect and grow wealth / Paul Nathan.
    p. cm.
    Includes bibliographical references and index.
    ISBN 978-1-118-04322-6 (cloth); ISBN 978-1-118-08421-2 (ebk);
    ISBN 978-1-118-08422-9 (ebk); ISBN 978-1-118-08423-6 (ebk)
        1. Gold standard—United States.   2. Gold—United States.   3. Investments—United States.   4. Monetary policy—United States.   5. Inflation (Finance)—United States.   I. Title.
    HG457.N37   2011
    332.4'2220973—dc22   2011005629

Printed in the United States of America

10   9   8   7   6   5   4   3   2   1

Dedicated to all those writers,
past and present,
who have helped make economics interesting and fun.

Contents

CONTENTS

Contents

Contents

Foreword

How is it that a book about gold, indeed a book that advocates a return to a gold standard, can sound so, well, reasonable?

Maybe it's because its author, Paul Nathan, is a very reasonable man. He's no gold bug. As far as I know he doesn't live in a fallout shelter. In fact he's an extraordinarily successful investor who came through the market crash of 2008–2009 smelling like a rose. You don't do that by being unreasonable.

Maybe it's also because there's nothing so unreasonable about gold. Maybe it's because what's unreasonable is saying that money ought to be just whipped up at the whims of government and not attached in any way to something of objective value—like gold.

From 1935 to 1975 it was illegal for Americans to own gold. The only exception was jewelry or dental fillings—relegating generations of Americans to the status of refugees or prisoners of war, reduced to hiding wealth in and about their bodies.

Gold is vilified by the political class and its servants in the profession of economics. The most famous economist of the twentieth century, John Maynard Keynes, called gold a "barbaric relic." Many scholars blame the gold standard of the years between the world wars for causing the Great Depression.

Yet I can't think of a single politician or economist who would turn down a bar of gold if you offered it to him. Indeed, every government in the world—the same governments whose printing presses churn out so much paper—all hoard gold for themselves.

The height of irony (perhaps *depth* would be a better word) is that the world's largest hoard of gold is stored in the basement of the Federal Reserve Bank of New York, a couple of blocks from the New York Stock Exchange.

I've seen it myself. You are taken by an armed guard five stories down into solid bedrock, 30 feet below the level of the New York subway system and 50 feet below sea level. You enter the vault through a person-sized slot revealed when a 90-ton steel cylinder is rotated. After you walk through the slot and the cylinder rotates back, you are in a watertight, airtight room half the size of a football field stacked to the roof with gold bricks weighing 27.4 pounds each.

At current prices this gold is worth more than $300 billion. There's more here than in Fort Knox. Almost all of it is held for foreign governments—very little of it is owned by the U.S. government (that's in Fort Knox), and none of it by individuals.

Gold is very dense. So each small bar is surprisingly heavy. Don't try holding one in just one hand. Vault workers wear ultrastrong magnesium shoe-covers to protect their feet from accidental drops that, over the years, have left the cement floor with dozens of deep dents.

The vault was built in 1921 and looks it. The technology is all very old-school. An enormous scale used to weigh gold bars, tons at a time, looks like a giant balance beam you'd expect to see in an antique apothecary shop—yet it is accurate within the weight of a grain of rice.

When you're in that vault, you know in your bones that there's nothing unreasonable about gold. It's not barbaric. It's not just a hunk of metal, assigned arbitrary value only by the whims of greedy nut-jobs like Auric Goldfinger. It's real wealth. It's real value. It's real money. It's just plain real.

After I visited the gold vault, I went upstairs for meetings with Federal Reserve officials to discuss monetary policy. Normally it's a rare privilege to talk to insiders about such market-moving matters. But after visiting the gold vault—after experiencing what real money feels like when you hold it in your own hands—all the talk about M2, the federal funds rate, and quantitative easing all seemed like nonsense.

It didn't help that on the way out of the vault my escort gave me a souvenir. No, it wasn't a gold bar. It was a little plastic bag, holding one ounce of shredded paper that had once been $100 bills.

After visiting the gold vault, it wouldn't have made any difference to me if those bills had not been shredded. They could have handed me intact $100 bills—and it would have still seemed like just paper.

It wouldn't have been gold. Which is to say, it wouldn't have been real.

When I was done I walked out onto the streets of New York. It was just beginning to rain, and vendors seemed to magically appear on street corners to sell umbrellas. At that moment an umbrella was a very precious thing to me and to thousands of others caught in the sudden rain. Yet these vendors were willing to accept, in exchange for one, a little piece of worn paper. Why weren't they demanding gold?

Would that have been so unreasonable?

Paul Nathan doesn't think so, and neither do I.

Chances are you don't, either. But maybe you don't have the words or the arguments to really crystallize your intuition. For you, then, this book will give articulate voice—it will apply reason—to what you already feel in your bones.

Some of you are skeptics about gold. This book could change your mind. Be reasonable. Read it.

There's one thing we can all agree on. Something has gone terribly wrong in the economic mechanism of the world. The terrible synchronized global recession we've just endured was a warning. How do we expect to recover, and how do we expect to avoid another financial crisis, if we don't do something to fix that mechanism?

Printing more paper money is probably not the answer. Paper money likely contributed to the problem. Hair of the dog that bit you can be a palliative but not a long-term strategy.

Would it be so unreasonable to at least think about giving a greater role to the medium of exchange and the store of value that has endured for centuries—gold?

Open up your mind, and let Paul Nathan try to convince you. What's in this book might just save the world.

DONALD L. LUSKIN
Chief Investment Officer, TrendMacro
Co-Author, *I Am John Galt*

Preface

As we entered the twenty-first century, we may have well entered the century of gold. For the first time in a very long time we are hearing talk about returning to a gold standard. Whether or not governments choose to move toward some form of gold standard is less important than the fact that the free market already is.

The world is in the process of rediscovering gold and is, in effect, moving toward a de facto gold standard, whether governments like it or not. No one can know for sure what shape this new gold standard will take, but given new technologies and the freedom of choice, it will at some point take on a life of its own. That is reason enough to strive to understand what a gold standard is and how it is different from the monetary system of today.

This book is not intended to portray gold or the gold standard as Utopian. There is no Utopia. However, the years, decades, and centuries of the gold standard, and gold itself as a store of value, have served mankind well. When I talk of the stability of the value of money over the centuries during the gold standard, I am not referring to the government-created money under the gold standard—such as the Continental, which was supposed to be as good as gold but ultimately became worthless. Nor am I talking about the suspension of gold convertibility by governments during that period, which amounts to a broken government promise.

I am not talking about the banks that backed their notes with gold and could not redeem them during panic runs due to imprudence or fraud. And I am not suggesting that gold will prevent, nor could have prevented, financial and credit crises from occurring; it certainly cannot prevent recessions and depressions. Yet, gold and the gold standard have been wrongly accused of causing many of these occurrences. They did not. Gold preserves wealth. The gold standard creates monetary stability. That is its great virtue. That is its legacy. Under the gold standard of the nineteenth century the dollar bought at the end of the century approximately what it bought at its beginning. At the end of the twentieth century, after going off the gold standard, the dollar bought 97 percent less!

While a pure gold standard has never existed in our history, the gold standard functioned effectively in various forms as the monetary system of the civilized world from roughly the early 1700s to 1913, when the Federal Reserve System took over the control of money and credit. As with "complete freedom" or "totally-free markets," a pure gold standard is an ideal. History has shown that— to the degree nations move toward these ideals of freedom, free markets, and sound money—people prosper. If there is one lesson that history has taught us, it is that money substitutes are merely promises. Every piece of paper that claims it is the equivalent of something else is a promise to pay. *Promises can be broken.* This should be painfully evident today after the Enron, WorldCom, AIG, and Lehman Brothers fiascos. Historically, it was never gold's "promise" that was broken. Gold traded as an honest equivalent against other commodities and services, as always, through good times and bad. It was the paper money claims that were always the root of lack of confidence and suspicion, often due to fraud and theft, leading to panics and crises.

When a government imposes legal tender laws compelling its citizens to accept paper claims, which amount to floating promises, then and only then, does money become tied to political promises rather than to the reality of the marketplace. Except for very rare occurrences, when the medium of exchange becomes unstable under the gold standard it is the money substitutes that are the problem—not the underlying commodity represented.

We live in a world of money substitutes called credit and debt. We are struggling to understand where we have gone wrong, why our institutions have failed us, how we should direct ourselves as a nation, and how to insure our financial futures against inflation, deflation, credit crises, debt defaults, panics, stock market plunges, and real estate declines. All good questions.

Where to start? Let's start at the beginning.

PAUL NATHAN

Part I

GOLD AND THE DOMESTIC ECONOMY

Chapter 1

Why Gold?

O ur infatuation with gold has been around as long as mankind itself. Some call it mystical; others call it a barbaric metal. It is a love-hate relationship that has survived the ages. To some it is blind love. To others it is the object of a great quest. Whatever its role in society, it has never been a benign one. It has never been a metal you ignore. We, to this day, refer to the very best of things as "the gold standard of. . . ." We call a great find a "gold mine" and claim something you can count on to be "as good as gold." We still "go for the gold" and present gold, silver, and bronze medals for achievement. When we hit our prime years, we call them "our golden years." Gold folklore and all of its history is embedded in our culture.

This tradition did not endure because the years of gold as money were tarnished. On the contrary, gold is as American as apple pie. But, among intellectuals, economists, and policy makers today, gold has a more mixed reputation.

Gold has been praised and denounced; called immaterial and impractical. At the same time it has been craved and adored. Governments have adopted gold as their money, denounced it, confiscated it, demonetized it, and hoarded it. Passions run high when it comes to gold. And so they should. One of the most contested and debated of all subjects is not just gold, but gold as money, gold as a standard of value, gold as an investment, and its role within our national and international monetary systems.

Gold: The King of Metals

Gold is a proven successful monetary standard because of its unique properties. Mankind has valued gold for 5,000 years. Through some 2,500 years of formalized monetary systems almost every conceivable commodity has been used as money: stones, tobacco, wheat, pottery, coconuts, beads, and bananas. After years of trial and error individuals selected precious metals as the premier money and gold rose to the top to become the king of metals. Why?

It wasn't an arbitrary choice. Gold is scarce, and in being so it is precious to individuals. It is easily identifiable. Nothing quite jumps out at you like the glitter of gold. Since it is easily recognizable it is easily marketable, which is essential to any medium of exchange. It is accepted by almost anyone anywhere in the world. It has utility. If need be it can be melted and used in various forms as a commodity—such as in the fields of dentistry, medicine, high tech, and others. The fact that it can be melted and utilized in various forms allows it to be made into rings, coins, ingots, or bars and used as money. Or it can be held as gold dust or nuggets. It's small in bulk and therefore portable. Artisans love it for its pliability and beauty. They use it in jewelry and use it in other art forms as well.

Whether as a commodity, money, jewelry, or art, gold has value to most individuals. It has become a way of storing value. It isn't perishable like tobacco or wheat. It doesn't evaporate or disintegrate. All of the gold in the world ever produced still exists. And because the total amount of gold above ground is always substantially greater than the supply that is found yearly, its supply remains stable year after year, century after century, in relation to other goods. Sudden changes of value are possible, but throughout history they are, like gold itself, very rare.

Gold Becomes the Standard of the World

The purchasing power of money under the gold standard, and the silver standard before it, remained fairly constant for over 200 years. Gold's price was fixed at $22.67 per ounce between the years 1792 to 1933, and the value of the dollar during that time was the same as an ounce of gold. During the years 1880 to 1914, the inflation rate was .01 percent. This 34-year period is known as the years of "the classical gold standard," when a dollar remained a dollar, and gave rise to the term "as good as gold." Since we have abandoned the gold standard the value of the dollar has fallen by 97 percent. The case for the gold standard and against the fiat standard is that simple and that strong.

Today, we prefer the virtues of paper. One of my favorite economists, Ludwig von Mises, once said, "Government is the only entity I know of that can take a perfectly good commodity like paper, slap some ink on it, and make it totally worthless." The same cannot be said for gold. Gold has withstood the test of time. Its virtues have been discovered and rediscovered throughout the years.

Our founding fathers went as far as declaring nothing but gold and silver shall be this nation's money. And in Europe it is common knowledge that "one should always have just enough gold to bribe the border guards." There are a lot of myths and misunderstandings about gold and its credibility as money. But once inspected, the myths pale next to the facts and documented history of gold. We will explore some of them now.

Too Little Gold—Or Too Much Paper?

Usually the first argument given by those that claim returning to a gold standard is impractical is that there isn't enough gold in the world to use for money. This argument makes more sense if you stand it on its head. It's not that there is too little gold—it's that there are too many paper dollars around, too many claims to gold.

First of all, it should be pointed out that during the gold standard there were never complaints of too little gold to use as money, even though both population and the amount of goods and services grew over its 200-year history. Tell people back in the nineteenth century that there was not enough gold to use as money and they would start looking at you sideways. Back then gold had been used as money for generations.

Banks were the major holders of gold. They kept about one quarter to one third of their capital in gold. They made loans based on their capital. A three- or four-to-one capital ratio was commonplace. Today it is closer to 14:1, and Lehman Brothers was said to have leveraged positions that exceeded 40:1. This kind of excessive leverage and inadequate capital contributed to the panic of 2008. During the gold standard, the amount of gold was leveraged—but only as long as it was redeemable on demand. Redemption placed limits on leverage.

Once the ratio has been determined, the prices of all things adjust and stability prevails. For every new ounce of gold discovered, four new dollars could be created. Throughout our history there has never been a time when there was too little gold to act as a medium of exchange. On the contrary, the gold strike of 1849 was more problematic than any problem arising from a shortage of gold, as the supply of money suddenly increased.

Secondly, other metals have been and can be used alongside gold. Silver, nickel, and copper all served as money during the gold standard. Those metals were also leveraged about four to one. As long as gold, silver, nickel, and copper circulate as coins, there is no reason that paper cannot also circulate as money substitutes, as long as they are at all times convertible on demand. The four to one capital ratio was not arbitrary. It was time tested and was deemed a safe ratio by markets in times of stability as well as times of panics and bank runs throughout the gold standard's existence to protect a bank against insolvency.

Today, the great debate the world is having is, "How much capital should banks maintain to prevent insolvency?" Stress tests are being conducted to determine that ratio. If governments would just look at the years of the gold standard they would have a model to emulate that is proven to have succeeded for centuries. We need not impose the exact same ratios, but an increase in capital and an increase in reserve requirements will do wonders to strengthen the banking system around the world.

The "Gold Prevents Prosperity" Myth

A companion argument to "There's not enough gold to be used for money" is that a gold standard is too rigid and restricts the expansion of business and therefore prosperity. This argument asserts that there is not enough gold to allow enough credit expansion to provide for a vigorous robust economy. This argument can be refuted with one simple historical fact: the industrial revolution. During the two centuries where the gold standard reigned, the world enjoyed the greatest amount of growth in mankind's history. The standard of living for the entire population of those nations tied to the gold standard rose to levels never before dreamed of. The world immersed itself in free trade and there was not a world war fought for a hundred years. And in the United States we transformed ourselves from an agrarian society to an industrial one. Those that claim that gold limits the amount of growth must have somehow missed this fact.

In the words of Nobel Prize winner Robert E. Lucas Jr., "The industrial revolution marks a major turning point in human history; almost every aspect of daily life was eventually influenced in some way. Most notably, average income and population began to exhibit unprecedented sustained growth. In the two centuries following 1800, the world's average per capita income increased over tenfold, while the world's population increased over sixfold. For the first time in history, the living standards of the masses of ordinary people have begun to undergo sustained growth. . . . Nothing remotely like this economic behavior has happened before."

No, gold does not prevent prosperity. It furthers it. For centuries this argument never ever occurred to people. Even though gold became relatively scarcer each year, during the industrial revolution, its value remained stable. There was always enough gold to serve as an effective medium of exchange. Only after we abandoned the gold standard did money claims become abundant rather than scarce and prices begin to rise progressively. The problem became a problem of not too *little* money but too *much* money. A term never heard before among common people emerged in the 20th century: inflation.

Those who argue that the gold standard is impractical because there is too little gold in circulation are overlooking what it means to have too many excess paper dollars in circulation. More paper dollars does not equate necessarily to more wealth. Many times just the opposite is true. I give you Zimbabwe as an example. According to the country's Central Statistic Office, the estimated rate of inflation rose to 11,200,000 percent in August of 2008. The Central bank introduced a new $10 billion note. Everyone had money. Except everyone was broke.

This is the illusion that can come with inflation. This is the illusion of having more money. The argument given that did away with the gold standard was that we needed an expanding monetary unit with less rigidity, one with greater flexibility. Once we did away with limitations on money and credit creation the result was a depreciation of the value of our dollar by 97 percent over the last century compared with the gold standard preserving 100 percent of its value the two centuries before. At the end of a century under the gold standard, one could buy a suit of clothes for approximately the same coins he did at the beginning of the century. Today we would have to drop a zero off our money to buy the same house we could have 40 years ago.

In Gold We Trust

We live in a time of great mistrust—mistrust of our banking system, of our debt, of our money, of our politicians, and our ability to return to a period of growth, prosperity, and stability. We live in a world of reckless government spending, fiscal irresponsibility, and trillions in unfunded liabilities. Until we correct these things, we need to deal with the monetary system as it is.

Interestingly, since the financial credit crisis, most would agree today that an increase in the capital requirements of financial institutions is a good thing and would have perhaps prevented the financial meltdown. A return to gold standard ratios is not out of the question given this realization. Adequate capital requirements and the subsequent decreased leverage they would bring are essential to the solvency of any monetary system.

The best we can hope for today is to improve the present system from within by making it more prudent and more honest. Financial reform would be best achieved by moving toward the operating principles of a gold standard. To build a better financial system we need to know what to aim for—what works, what doesn't, and why. Gold represents a two-century history lesson in which the value of money remained constant. This is something no other monetary system can claim.

The years in which gold, silver, nickel, and copper were used as money represent years of growth, prosperity, and relative stability. The gold standard does not claim to eliminate panics, crises, greed, or irrationality. But it does guarantee that the purchasing power of money will be preserved as long as the rules of the gold standard are adhered to.

Why Gold?

The rules of the gold standard come from the natural automatic flows of money and trade between individuals throughout the world; from a government committed to defending the value of its currency; through the certainty of convertibility of paper money to a commodity at a fixed ratio. The rules require both free trade and fiscal discipline. To exist, a gold standard requires a system of limited government, limited spending, limited debt and credit creation, and the protection of individual and property rights under the law.

Why gold? Because gold is a time-honored and time-tested honest currency. It establishes a system based on financial, monetary, and fiscal discipline. Today's fiat standard is barely a century old and may not make it to its hundredth birthday. My guess is that if it does, it will be with the help of gold, or at least by moving toward the principles of sound money and the discipline that a gold standard requires. Without these, financial reform efforts will be meaningless. No paper money system can survive without them. None ever have.

Chapter 2

The Gold Standard: A Standard for Freedom*

At one time the case for the gold standard was practically self-evident—undisputed by most economists and appreciated by both laymen and professionals. Today, however, the case for gold is buried under decades of propaganda, misconceptions, and myths. It has been only recently that the case for the gold standard has begun to surface from under the policy makers' anti-gold debris. Consequently, gold is once again gaining the attention and interest it so rightly deserves.

---

*This article is a reprint from *The Freeman*, published by The Foundation for Economic Education in January 1975, the year gold was once again made legal in the United States.

13

Today's free-market advocates of the gold standard differ from past advocates. For example, free-market advocates do not exclude silver or other commodities from their concept of a gold standard. Indeed, they do not even insist that gold must be money. The case for the gold standard is actually the case for market-originated commodity money, and the case against government-regulated fiat money. It is simply an extension of the case for free markets that respect the rights of individuals, and the case against controlled markets that violate the rights of individuals.

To be concerned with the gold standard is to be concerned with a free economy, regulated by the values and choices of individuals, rather than a controlled economy in which the values and choices of individuals are regulated by government. This concern for an individual's freedom to express values and exercise choices is derived from a deeper concern for justice and for an individual's right to property. The individual concerned with justice does not aim to force others to use gold as money. Rather, he insists that government has no right to prevent him and other individuals from using gold as money if they choose. The individual concerned with property rights does not urge government to legislate pro-gold policies in order to arbitrarily increase the value, popularity, or status of gold. Rather, he insists that government stop inflating, since this arbitrarily decreases the value of his monetary claims to property.

Antagonists of the gold standard claim that it is impractical. They cite such myths as we have too little gold, and gold restricts prosperity, while ignoring the virtues and history of the gold standard. But the gold standard is, in fact, the most practical monetary system yet conceived by individuals. However, the gold standard's primary virtue does not lie in its practicality: It lies in its morality. Those concerned about such things as freedom, justice, the preservation of property rights and purchasing power, would do well to consider the moral case for the gold standard, for, once understood, it is the individual's best defense against government confiscation of property through inflation.

The fact that prevents a government from indulging in inflationary schemes under the gold standard can be best summed up in a phrase: governments can't print gold. But to understand the implications of this statement, and the virtues of having gold as money, it is first necessary to understand what money is—and what money is not.

What Money Is . . .

An individual on a deserted island has no need for money. He produces the goods he needs to survive, and consumes all he produces. Similarly, a primitive society has no need for money. The kinds of goods produced are extremely limited, and if individuals desire to exchange their goods with one another, they can do so through direct exchange, such as barter. But under a division-of-labor economy, where individuals specialize in production and where there is a variety of goods produced, desired, and traded, there is a very definite need for money. For how else could Mr. Jones in Florida sell his oranges to individuals throughout the world and then buy Mr. Smith's bestselling novel, unless there existed some medium of exchange acceptable to all parties?

Money originates from individual's desire for indirect exchange. And more, since indirect exchange usually occurs between strangers like Smith and Jones, money must be an object that is mutually valued. Thus, money is that commodity that serves as a medium of exchange by virtue of its high degree of marketability.

The task of discovering which commodity will be most valued by and most acceptable to individuals as a medium of exchange can only be accomplished through a market process; for it is only through the market that individual's values and choices are properly reflected. The verdict of the market has reflected three general requirements for any lasting medium of exchange: that money should be generally acceptable to most individuals; that it should be practical to use; and that it should be relatively stable in value. If these requirements are satisfied, the result is a money of trust.

Trust is the lifeblood of money, and money is the lifeblood of any economy based on the indirect exchange of goods and services. A currency of trust serves to facilitate exchange among individuals and, in doing so, breeds a healthy and growing economy. But if individuals begin to mistrust money, the market immediately reflects this loss of confidence. Then money begins to lose stability, lose its acceptability, and soon becomes impractical to use in exchange.

Mistrusted money is the antithesis of the lifeblood of an economy. It's a kind of "bad blood" circulating between individuals throughout the economy, breeding confusion and suspicion. The fact that individuals' mistrust of money will result in monetary crises and collapse, underscores the need for a money that never contradicts individuals' values, a money that at all times properly reflects individuals' values; that is, a money based on, and constantly exposed to, individual choices—which means a free-market-originated commodity money.

When one considers the complex process that must take place before individuals can discover which commodity money constantly reflects their changing values and choices, one can understand why it is only through a free-market process that money can properly evolve as a medium of trust. And one may also understand why no individual, group of individuals, or government has the right to dictate what money or its value should be. This decision must be a market decision if it is to be a lasting decision.

Throughout history, almost every conceivable commodity has been used as a medium of exchange. Through the years of economic development and through trial and error, those commodities least suited to serve as money were eliminated, while those commodities best suited survived as forms of money. After centuries of exchange between individuals, the commodity that emerged as the most valued, the most practical, the most trusted money among individuals, was gold.

What gives rise to individual's trust in gold? First, individuals value gold as money because individuals value gold as a commodity. Gold at any time can be converted to its commodity role if its monetary role should ever be questioned. Second, since gold is relatively scarce and precious to individuals, it has stability of value. Therefore, it can be trusted to serve as a relatively stable medium of exchange. And since most individuals desire to save part of what they produce in some monetary form, gold's stability of value provides them with a reliable monetary method of accumulating and storing wealth.

What else gives rise to individual's trust in gold? Gold is easily marketable, which means it is acceptable to individuals in exchanges of all kinds. Gold is also trusted because it is practical: it's durable, so it won't perish or rot; it's small in bulk, so it is easily transportable. It's a metal, which means it can be used in different forms, such as bars or coins; and, since gold does not evaporate, it will lose neither quantity nor quality if or when individuals should decide to melt their coins into bullion or melt their bullion for use in production.

There is one more thing that gives rise to individual's trust in gold: the knowledge that gold cannot be counterfeited; the conviction that the money supply cannot be artificially and arbitrarily increased by those who would aim to confiscate wealth rather than produce it; the knowledge that money (the claim to production and effort) will itself represent production and effort. In short, individual's trust in gold carries the conviction that the monetary system freely adopted by individuals is based, not on whim and decree, but on integrity and productivity.

These are some of the reasons why individuals have trusted gold as a medium of exchange through history—and why today's policy makers do not.

. . . And What Money Is Not

Money is not paper. Paper notes evolve from the desire for a convenient substitute for commodity money. The paper notes that circulate as money today were once money substitutes (receipts for gold), defined by and convertible into a specific amount of gold. Paper notes did not and cannot become a money of trust without first representing a commodity of trust.

Consider the reaction of free individuals—individuals who, understanding and respecting the meaning of property rights, are suddenly and for the first time offered in place of gold, non-convertible paper notes. These notes would be meaningless to such individuals. No individual who had just come from harvesting a field of wheat would even consider trading his wheat for scrap paper.

There are only two ways in which individuals will accept paper notes without commodity convertibility: if they are forced to do so or if they are conned into doing so. Americans are now legally forced to accept government's nonconvertible paper notes—but only because they have been conned into believing that commodity money is old-fashioned and impractical and that paper notes are indicative of a modern and sophisticated economy.

Nothing could be further from the truth. Nonconvertible paper "money" is fiat money that derives its value, not from its value as a commodity, not from its value as a useful medium of exchange according to the requirements of a medium of exchange, but from the decree of government. Fiat money is a throwback to the days of kings and the mentality of dictators. It is not a money evolved from the values and choices of free individuals in free markets but a money created through the coercion of government.

Is commodity money old-fashioned and impractical, as today's policy makers contend it is? Consider the following facts: Over the last several decades, the exchange ratios (the prices) of various commodities have not varied much in value relative to each other. For example, the value of eggs to milk or milk to bread would be at approximately the same ratios today as they were years ago.

But if it is true that the exchange ratios of commodities are relatively the same today as they were in the past, why then have prices (the exchange ratios of dollars to goods) soared over the years? The reason is that the value of the paper money, with which government forces everyone to deal, has fallen yearly relative to all commodities. Clearly, if a commodity (theoretically, almost any commodity) had been used as a medium of exchange over the past decades instead of government's fiat money, prices would have remained relatively stable. It is important to realize that it is not commodities that are rising in value, but fiat money that is falling in value.

Since 1933, when the United States severed the dollar-commodity relationship by abandoning what was left of the gold standard, the value of the dollar has depreciated by over two-thirds in relation to other commodities. This could never occur under a commodity standard—only under a government imposed fiat standard. Had the United States returned to a dollar based on and convertible into gold instead of severing the dollar to gold relationship, the supply of dollars over the years would have been limited to, or checked by, the supply of gold. Therefore, the value of the dollar today would have been equal to the value of gold in relation to other commodities. Instead, the United States decided to print dollars whenever "needed" and to pretend that the dollar was "as good as gold" by legally fixing its value. The pretense couldn't last, and today the dollar is worth a fraction of its value. In 1933 it was fixed at $35 per ounce. That is a fraction of its present price today.

Paper notes that are not representative of and convertible into a commodity are not money and have never satisfied the requirements of money for long. They are notes of circulating debt which individuals are forced to accept, so that governments can continuously pursue their policies of inflationary finance. This enables them to grow government and spend at will. A gold standard restricts government spending, and it is this that politicians object to strenuously.

The Nature of Inflation

Inflation is the fraudulent increase in the supply of money substitutes and credit. It is a policy that allows government to artificially create and spend more money than it is able to collect in taxes or borrow from its citizens. Government is the cause of inflation—the effect is higher prices.

Consider each dollar as a claim to some tangible good. If the claims are increased, the value of each claim goes down because there are more dollars seeking goods. This bids prices up.

But inflation is not simply rising prices. In fact, inflation may exist even when prices remain the same or decrease. How is this possible? If the production of goods and services increases more than the artificial increase in paper claims, prices will drop—but not by as much as they would have, had there been no artificial increase in paper claims. Thus, in real terms, the value of paper claims is effectively reduced even though in relative terms the value of these claims may increase.

Historically, and in relatively free market economies, there are only two ways in which a general across-the-board increase in prices can occur: through a dramatic increase in commodity money (such as new gold discoveries) or through a fraudulent increase of money substitutes by banks and governments. The former type of general price increase rarely occurs and is perfectly natural. The latter is both unnatural and immoral.

In the case of new gold production, those who have produced the new commodity money will have earned the right to exchange their product for the products of others. All other non-money producers may have to pay higher prices for goods, as the supply of gold increases, but the higher prices are compensated for by having more money to spend. Who receives the "new" money will depend on individual productivity—and this is as it should be: the justice of the market is that the acquisition and distribution of wealth is based upon productivity rather than decree.

But, given a fiat standard where government sanctions and sponsors an artificial increase in paper money or credit, the increase in purchasing power for some individuals can only be obtained at the expense of other individuals. Given a fiat standard, income distribution is the result of chance, caprice, or government favors and loans. When government doles out its fiat money, these notes dilute the value of all other outstanding money claims. Those who receive the fiat money first benefit from spending their money before prices rise. But as the fiat money is spent, prices are higher for all other consumers. Thus, the difference between a real increase in the money supply (i.e., commodity money) and an artificial increase (i.e., in paper claims) is the difference between production and theft.

Clearly, inflation is a moral issue. However prices respond, it is immoral that some individual, agency, or government is legally permitted to obtain wealth at the involuntary expense of other individuals. The major challenge in the sphere of monetary relations today is how to abolish the coercive power of government to control the supply and regulate the value of money, and how to return this function to the market where it properly belongs.

The Fiat Standard at Work

Under a fiat standard, government gains control of the banking system and thus, indirectly, of the nation's money supply. It can artificially and arbitrarily create money and furnish credit. Government paper notes are not based on nor are they convertible into gold or any other tangible commodity. An individual's production and labor are not the sole claim to other individual's production and labor: government determines the supply and value of money.

Under the American version of the fiat standard, the banking system and the nation's money supply are controlled and regulated for the most part by a 12-person Board of Governors, which is empowered to make policy decisions for the majority of the nation's banks. Thus, America's banking system is not a free and private banking system—it is a quasi-governmental banking system, known as the Federal Reserve System (referred to hereafter as the Fed).

It should be clear that the Fed's power to create claims against individuals' property is immoral. But neither the Fed nor the fiat standard is ever defended on moral grounds; they are defended on practical grounds. Once inspected, however, these grounds turn out to be about as solid as quicksand. The primary justification given for a fiat standard is that credit can be extended far more rapidly and extensively. This, it is claimed, is the fiat standard's major virtue. It is, in fact, a major vice.

The greatest economic threat under a fiat standard is that the Fed will supply heavy doses of money and credit to the loan market in an attempt to reduce interest rates and stimulate the economy. This attempt, while temporarily stimulating economic activity, leads to malinvestment, as business people falsely anticipate greater profits. A boom results, but since the boom is artificially created, the prosperity is temporary and, for the most part, illusory.

Government has not furnished more goods; it has not increased the nation's prosperity; it has simply increased the money supply— which leads people to believe they are richer. The fact is, however, they only have more paper claims to goods. This cannot enrich anyone and can only lead to future inflation; that is, a reduction of the value of real claims to wealth.

The Illusion of Prosperity

Thus, increases of money and credit provide only an illusion of prosperity, for with increased money and credit come increased costs for producer goods and increased wage costs. Higher wages then lead to overconsumption, as consumers, too, are enticed by the illusion of prosperity. But overconsumption results in higher prices, which reduce the consumer's standard of living. Since the boom was inflation-inspired, producers and consumers are not better off—they are worse off. Malinvestment and over-consumption are mistakes—errors in judgment—caused by government's attempt to con its citizens into believing that profit opportunities are better than they really are.

When the credit expansion that stimulated the boom ends, the mistakes that were made cannot be perpetuated. These mistakes must be liquidated: consumers buy less and begin paying off their unrealistic accumulation of debts. Producers liquidate inventories. Interest rates rise, and unemployment increases as the economy struggles to readjust. The severity of the readjustment depends on the degree and length of government's prior credit expansion and the policies implemented to cope with the adverse effects. Given continual injections of money and credit in the inane attempt to continue the boom and prevent a necessary recession, hyperinflation will result. Hyperinflation must lead to monetary chaos as well as economic disaster; that is, to depression. A major depression is not a necessary result of the fiat standard, but inflation and the boom-bust cycles are.

The whole purpose of fiat money is to allow government to spend more money than it can raise in direct taxes from its citizens. As a result, the American fiat standard has worked more often as a means of redistributing wealth than a means of stimulating the economy. Government, instead of furnishing money to the loan market in the attempt to continuously reduce interest rates, has created money to finance the welfare state. When government's fiat money enters the economy in the form of checks for expenditures, rather than through the loan market, the sequence of events and the effects are a little different.

Individuals usually hold their money as savings, but as prices continue to rise over the years of government deficit spending, individuals realize that the pieces of paper they hold are continuously and progressively depreciating in value—that inflation is becoming a way of life. Once individuals begin to lose confidence in government's fiat money, it's only a matter of time before the years of simple inflation burst into hyperinflation and monetary collapse.

Whether government tries to stimulate the economy or to finance programs that it cannot afford, the fiat standard is self-defeating and counterproductive. The consequences of America's fiat standard have been mild by historical standards: the Great Depression of the 1930s, an endless series of booms and busts since then, and a depreciation of the dollar to a fraction of its former value. So much for the practicality of the fiat standard!

The Meaning of the Gold Standard

In a free society, no individual, group of individuals, or government has the right to infringe upon the rights of others. This means that within a free society, the initiation of force is banned. All goals must be attained through persuasion and voluntary cooperation, and no goal may be achieved at the expense of any individual—not for the good of another individual, not for the good of the state, and not for the good of society. A system of voluntary exchange is a system of laissez-faire capitalism. Under capitalism, the individuals' rights are supreme. These rights are defended by government—not violated by government.

A gold standard is an integral part of a free society; a fiat standard is an integral part of a controlled society. A gold standard cannot exist without the consent of individuals; a fiat standard cannot exist without the initiated force of government. A gold standard is based on voluntary exchange, the recognition of individual's values, and respect for private property; a fiat standard is based on compulsory exchange, the denial of individual's values, and the insidious confiscation of private property.

Wealth is production, and gold is the equivalent of wealth produced. Because neither wealth nor gold can be created out of nothing, neither wealth nor gold are possible without individuals of intelligence, individuals of ability, and individuals of productivity. Fiat is force and it is the equivalent of wealth confiscated. Both fiat and force are the tools of those that seek the unearned.

Where a gold standard is welcomed by productive and honest individuals, the fiat standard is welcomed by those that prefer government control and regulation. Where the gold standard demands the earned, the fiat standard grants the unearned. Where a gold standard evolves from individual choice, a fiat standard evolves from government edict. Where a gold standard necessitates only that individuals be left free to act, to choose, and to trade, a fiat standard invites government to control, to regulate, and to dictate individuals' choices, actions, and the terms of trade.

Gold limits the government's power to spend more money than it receives in taxes and, in doing so, gold limits the government's arbitrary power over the economy; gold checks artificial money and credit expansion; it prevents artificial booms, which lead to very real busts; gold protects individuals from economically unsound government programs; and it protects citizens from the inflationary confiscation of private property. Not only is the gold standard the most practical monetary system yet discovered, it is a standard consistent with freedom—yet it is the gold standard that today's policy makers either ignore or denounce.

Chapter 3

Why Prices Have Not Skyrocketed

It is common knowledge that the Fed created huge sums of money in order to shore up the balance sheets of financial institutions during the recent financial crisis. The assumption by many then as now is that this would lead to a burst of inflation. So, why aren't prices skyrocketing?

For the purpose of this discussion I will define inflation as too much money chasing too few goods, resulting in an across-the-board increase in prices. Credit is a derivative of money and must also be considered since it also has a claim on goods. Deflation would be the exact opposite: Too little money and credit chasing too many goods, leading to falling prices. Milton Friedman originated the definition, more as a way of simplifying an understanding of inflation for the layman than as a serious theory of the value of money. That he did elsewhere.

The Quantity Theory of Money, or monetarism, is the accepted monetary theory of our day. Most investors, economists, and political pundits, and probably you yourself, hold that a major increase in money and credit is inflationary and will inevitably lead to higher prices. Irving Fisher formalized the theory in the 1920s and Milton Friedman expounded on the theory in the 1970s. Friedman's clear and simple way of explaining the nature of inflation was grasped easily by professionals and laymen alike. Milton Friedman almost single-handedly waged and won the war against inflation during the 1970s, a period when we needed him most. But I am not a monetarist. Monetarism is not wrong; it is simply incomplete.

On Human Action

There is another theory of money that challenges the monetarists' theory of money that I believe makes a lot more sense—one that explains why we are not experiencing a lot higher prices given the huge increase in the money supply. It is the Subjective Theory of Value, as formalized by Ludwig von Mises and the Austrian School of Economics. This theory holds, in its simplest form, that money derives its value not from the quantity in circulation but from the value individuals place on money in exchange for other goods.

What always leads to price rises or price declines is the hoarding or dishoarding of money by the population at large. Increases in the money supply can influence the value people place on money but it is only one factor in calculating the future value of money. The monetarist school sees an increase in money as a cause of higher prices, where the Austrian school does not. In the end it is the actions individuals take themselves based on their value of money that lead to higher prices, according to the Austrian school.

If Ben Bernanke dropped dollars from helicopters tomorrow, Friedman would say that inflation would result. Von Mises would say it would depend on what individuals did with the money and to what degree. If they put it under their mattress no increase in prices would occur. If they spent it, monetarists would compute the amount of the increase in new money and predict an inflation rate based on the percentage of increase in the quantity of money. Von Mises would suggest that it is just as likely that all money previously created would lose value as individuals lose confidence in all paper claims that serve as a medium of exchange. He, I believe, would conclude that hyperinflation was more possible than progressive inflation; that a breakdown of the monetary system would be more likely than a discounting of the value of money leading to progressively higher prices. Zimbabwe is a good example of that.

ssAt any time individuals decide to suddenly save rather than spend, prices tend to fall regardless of the quantity of money in circulation. Whenever individuals decide to increase their spending sharply and suddenly, prices tend to rise. The monetarist theory of money only partially explains the phenomenon of inflation and deflation. It was very correct in the 1970s within that particular context. It is not doing so well in present-day America as the context has completely changed.

In the 1970s the Federal Reserve System printed vast amounts of money that went directly into consumption. Today the Fed has printed vast amounts of money that has gone directly into savings by individuals, businesses, and financial institutions. The Fed dramatically increased the money supply beginning in September 2008. According to Friedman, prices should respond within 9 to 12 months. So we should have seen a marked increase in prices by the fourth quarter of 2009. We did not. In January we saw a 2.6 percent year over year increase in the Consumer Price Index (CPI) and the core rate actually declined for the first time since the early eighties. One year later, in the first quarter of 2010, we actually saw prices fall. For all of 2010, inflation is coming in at one of the lowest levels in history.

Many economists suggest that we do not have an inflation problem now but we will a year or two from now. I know of no theory that can project prices several years in advance. Those that are suggesting higher prices are inevitable sometime in the future are simply guessing. There is no causal link. The fact is, the money supply was increased more during 2008 than ever before in history. Yet, inflation has remained low.

Those who argue that prices will rise sharply in the future are actually saying that when the money that the Fed printed begins to be used for consumption, we will have an inflationary problem. This would be true if and when it happens. But this is the Austrian school's view of the world, not the monetarist school.

If all of a sudden, for whatever reason, people begin to dishoard money, its value will fall and prices will rise. It is human action that dictates prices, not the quantity of money. Most people point to gold and other hard commodities versus fiat money all over the world over the last many years as signs of inflation. The value of most currencies has fallen in relation to gold as individuals dishoard paper money and hoard gold and most other commodities. But this is not inflation.

Consumer prices have remained stable. That is because the new money created is not chasing goods. Fiat money has been targeted towards gold and other assets. This suggests that an increase in the money supply is "not always and everywhere" inflationary. It does not always lead to a general across the board increase in prices. It may show up elsewhere such as stocks, real estate, or commodities—or it may not show up at all.

The Subjective Theory of Value does not dispute the fact that if a government prints up progressively more and more money and throws it into circulation the monetary unit will probably fall in value. It usually does—but not always. The cause and effect is not one of increased money equals increased prices. It is a change in human action that values money less that leads to increased prices.

Quantity versus Values

The distinction is an important one and goes to the heart of today's monetary argument. Is inflation based on the single act of increasing the money supply? Or is it based on how individuals perceive its increase and how they act on it? I come down on the side of von Mises on the subject. If a majority of people today believed their money was going to depreciate by 50 percent next year in terms of goods, in my book (or should I say von Mises' book—which happens to be called *Human Action*), they would begin discounting the monetary unit today. My conclusion is that they do not believe that. Prices have risen in the last year, but there is no panic out of currencies in relation to goods. And interest rates, the price of money, have remained stable rather than soaring to discount future depreciation.

Monetarists will argue that it is just a matter of time and the newly printed money will eventually start chasing goods and bid up prices. Yet, that is not the expectation of the markets. Markets know there is not too much money or credit chasing too few goods. The bond market confirms this and long-term inflationary expectations have remained in check. This could all change in a matter of minutes, but it would not have to do with the quantity of money. If prices did begin to increase dramatically, a vast increase in the quantity of money could not be the trigger—that trigger has already been pulled. It would be due to a sudden change in individual perceptions of the value of money going forward—and this is never predictable. The big difference between monetarism and the Subjective Theory of Value is the first believes it can predict inflation or deflation. The latter knows it cannot.

The Quantity of Money and the Gold Standard

Even during the gold standard there was inflation and deflation. It was usually due to unexpected gold strikes or unexpected economic contractions. The gold standard served the nations of the world well for centuries. Money remained fairly stable. There were many sharp recessions but they were over quickly and they were within the context of continuous and dynamic growth. The years of the gold standard were the years of the industrial revolution.

Sir Isaac Newton, one of the smartest men who ever lived, helped establish and preserve the gold standard during the mid 1600s. Some of the greatest minds in England's seventeenth century, such as Adam Smith and John Locke, continued to champion the gold standard that ushered in the British industrial revolution. The Founding Fathers, no slouches in their own right, established the gold standard as the monetary system of the United States of America and wrote it into the U.S. Constitution. It was the monetary system that led to the American industrial revolution. But

Woodrow Wilson ignored the advice of world-renowned economists; he discarded the gold standard and replaced it with the edicts of the Federal Reserve Board.

You don't have a monetary system that lasts centuries because it is ineffective. True, we had a lot of normal economic ups and downs, but the worst of those downturns lasted only a short time, not a decade as did the Great Depression or the malaise of the 1970s. More importantly, the value of money always stayed fairly constant during those years, which is all that the gold standard guarantees. It never guaranteed economic Utopia. Under the fiat standard we have lost 97 percent of our money's value since the government replaced the gold standard with the Fed and to this day we still have panics and severe recessions.

For sure, we know that in all things monetary and economic, context changes and today is no exception. Today, I am less concerned about progressive inflation and more concerned that the fiat standard we have established is failing. Many are calling for fundamental monetary reform. But, from this point it would be easier to improve the fiat system than to replace it. Fiat currencies all over the world are losing confidence. Gold is reflecting this.

A medium of exchange must be a medium of trust to be a lasting medium. Money must be dependable. The artificial increase in the money supply by governments undercuts that trust. This is the case today. But it is not the Fed that is the real threat; it is irresponsible politicians in general.

Too Little Fiscal Responsibility Chasing Too Many Politicians

Inflation has been held in check by the knowledge that money can be pulled out of the system as fast as need be under a fiat standard. The real threat is the viability of the entire world fiat system.

If trust is to be regained in the system it needs to start with fiscal responsibility. Monetary policy is far easier to control by an independent authority than is government spending by a world of spendthrift politicians. The debt that has been created by most nations today is a far greater threat to the global economy than the threat of inflation. Monetary reform is required, I agree, but not today. It is fiscal reform that is required.

No monetary system, neither the fiat standard nor the gold standard, can survive reckless tax and spending policies by government. Our first task is not fighting inflation. Our first task is to rein in deficit spending and address unfunded liabilities. Without addressing those problems a mere increase in prices—or decrease—is dwarfed by the potential of a prolonged recession, such as has occurred in Japan over the last two decades, and the toll that would take on this country. Or worse, a chain reaction of debt defaults that could bring the entire international monetary system tumbling down.

It is important to keep an eye on inflation, and deflation, and the Fed, and the dollar. But I suggest that we as a nation, indeed, we as a world, need to sharpen our focus and deal immediately with government spending, government debt, government entitlements, and tax policy. Long before any action need be taken on monetary reform to rein in inflation we need to address our fiscal problems. No monetary reform will be meaningful or lasting without fiscal sanity. I suggest we stop wagging our fingers at the Fed and redirect them toward those that want to spend more on government programs with no way of paying for them.

Chapter 4

The Inflation/Deflation Conundrum

B ack in the 1970s everyone defined inflation as an increase in prices. Milton Friedman convinced the public and the pundits that we needed to look at the cause of inflation instead of the effects, which Friedman defined as "an excessive increase in the supply of money."

Today, everyone cites the Friedman definition. But they have lost sight of the whole definition, that is inflation is "an excessive increase in the supply of money that leads to *an across-the-board increase in prices.*" This definition contains both cause and effect. The Austrian School of monetary theory disagrees with this definition. It holds it is the hoarding and dishoarding of money that leads to inflation and deflation. I agree, and I think that theory is being proved today. But, it is the monetarist definition that is most widely accepted, so we will use it here.

A statement uttered so often today is "We have both inflation and deflation going on at the same time." Do we? The answer is obviously no—if you define your terms. By definition it is impossible to have both an increase and a decrease in the nation's money supply at the same time. And it is impossible to have an across-the-board increase and across-the-board decrease in prices at the same time. That's the short answer. The long answer is a little more interesting. Let's put the monetarist theories and Austrian classical theories aside for a moment. Let's do what economists tell laymen never to do. Let's look at the meaning of the question in the vernacular.

We live in a world where the prices of some things are noticeably rising and others are falling. This is where we get the vernacular expressions of "commodity inflation," and "real estate deflation," and "energy inflation," and "technology deflation," and "food inflation," and so on. But we are not experiencing an across-the-board progressive increase in prices. We have not experienced a significant across-the-board increase in inflation in thirty years. The Consumer Price Index (CPI) has in fact fallen from rates of 14 percent to under 1 percent during that period. We have had what might be called "progressive disinflation."

Some argue that the indexes that measure inflation are wrong. I have news for these folks. They are always wrong—no matter which index you use, it must be wrong by its nature. There cannot be an index that properly measures all prices and their cross-relationships at a single moment of time. We subjectively choose a method of measurement and that is our yardstick—and there are many of them with many different types of goods, weightings, and compensations. Soon there will be a Google CPI. It will comprise all of the retail prices within the Google universe, priced on a minute-by-minute basis. It will also be wrong. Here's the problem.

If you are in the home industry as a contractor, a builder, a construction worker, a real estate agent, appraiser, or mortgage lender, you live in a world of deflation, where the price of what you sell has been going down, together with the income you have been receiving. If you are a miner, or selling or buying commodities, or in the farming or agriculture business, you live in an inflationary world. If you export anything nowadays, you live in an inflationary-booming world where price increases are routine and dramatic, and unemployment has been running only in the 3 to 4 percent range. So, where you live, and which part of the economy you work in, determines whether you are experiencing inflation or deflation. That is what is meant by those who say we are experiencing inflation and deflation at the same time. Thus, inflation becomes an acutely personal matter.

The job of an economist, however, is to determine what is going on with the economy as a whole. Terminology such as the above only serves to confuse things. If monetary policy is stable, when prices go up in one area, they must fall in another area. We cannot have gasoline inflation without having less money to spend somewhere else. We cannot have food inflation without it costing us more and having less to spend on other things. In an evenly rotating economy we always will have some prices rising and others falling. So, there is nothing unusual about the statement. Increasing and decreasing prices in a market economy is the norm. And that is just what we have had for the last 30 years. It is only when we have progressively increasing amounts of money being printed that we can have the phenomenon known as inflation—a progressive across-the-board increase in prices.

The Cause of the Recent Spike in Commodities

Now, there is a secondary argument made that is important to look at. That is the statement that it is only the things we need or really want that are going up, not the things that are less important. Gold and silver are perfect examples. They are precious metals. At $1,400 gold, people have to pay a lot more for their precious ounce of gold than when it was $35 an ounce in the 1970s. And that silver dollar you had in your pocket in 1967 will buy about $30 worth of goods today. What changed?

Well, money supply increased dramatically throughout the twentieth century—that is for sure. But, something else has changed recently that has led to an unusual run-up of some commodity prices in particular, many to all-time highs. Because some governments continuously practice protectionism, dollars have piled up in their treasuries and are not being allowed to flow back. These governments prevent their citizens from freely importing other nation's goods. This has caused huge imbalances.

Under the automatic rules of the gold standard, money was free to flow from nation to nation, and did so for centuries. As money flowed into a nation its money supply would increase and prices would rise. The exact opposite occurred in the nation where money flowed out—prices would fall.

As this occurred, those who saw cheaper goods become available abroad would begin buying those goods instead of domestic goods and the entire process would reverse itself. It was like a teeter-totter. The result was a world in constant movement toward equilibrium. No government intervention was required. Balance was constantly being restored automatically due to free markets and free trade.

That is not the case today. Today, we have Sovereign Wealth Funds, as an arm of governments who wish to get rid of their surpluses. They are going after commodities—and strategic commodities at that. Oil is being stockpiled along with things like copper, gold, silver, cotton, sugar, and anything that is of importance to that particular government and nation. It is a government-led demand, not a consumer-led demand.

This has added to today's price imbalances and distortions as dollars have been concentrated and focused on particular commodities that governments want. It is one thing for dollars to come back from China seeking an array of consumer products that individuals want. It is quite another thing for a fund set up by a government to go around the world buying up scarce resources. If the American government were to do this, all hell would break loose! In this country, the American government is not the major purchaser; the consumer is.

Add Exchange Traded Funds (ETFs), which track and/or accumulate commodities, to this artificial government-created demand, and you add another source of demand by investors throughout the world. Finally, this is trickling down to the average citizen who is recognizing that if there is something he or she really needs or wants, he or she better get it now before it is entirely out of reach or its availability disappears completely. Is this inflation? No. It's called "hoarding."

The endgame, as they say, is a run on particular goods that are scarce and/or necessary to live. Food, energy, and strategic metals, are among the goods being sought. Gold and silver are being accumulated as the ultimate medium of exchange to trade for precious goods. Prices of metals, collectibles, antiques, exotic cars, certain wines, rare works of art, oil, and food, are all going through the roof.

So, it is fair to say we are experiencing a surge in prices of those things we really need or want. But, as long as the money supply increases remain stable, we pay for these things at the expense of other things, forcing those prices down. This is the cause of the inflation/deflation conundrum. This is the world we are living in and will be living in for some time to come. It is a world of protectionism, unending trade surpluses, and price imbalances—all leading to hoarding.

The solution is free trade, free markets, and eventually a universal monetary system based on confidence; a monetary system based on stability and predictability; a system based on the free flow of money among citizens throughout the world. This kind of system requires a lot more freedom, a lot less government, and objective rules that are adhered to by governments. It is a system that is attainable. It is a system that rested on the two pillars of free market capitalism and free trade, and it has existed and served mankind well for centuries: It was the gold standard.

Chapter 5

Central Banking in the Twenty-First Century

The Fed was created in 1913, along with dozens of other government regulatory agencies in a wave of populism spearheaded by President Woodrow Wilson. It was a time when the public was rebelling against wealthy captains of industry for becoming too rich. It was a time when the policies of regulation and control were institutionalized to replace the functions of the free market. It was a time very much like today. The fact that the free market had just produced an industrial revolution that led to the highest standard of living individuals and the world had ever known escaped the wisdom of the masses. To them the industrial revolution became unimportant compared to the more popular cries for social justice. In the end they would receive neither.

The Fed was created to protect individuals against the discipline and harshness of capitalism and the gold standard. It took the United States off the gold standard that had lasted since America's inception. The industrial revolution was built upon the gold standard and the reliability of sound money. The Fed could instead create paper money at will. The Constitution explicitly states that only specie, which means commodities like gold and silver and nickel and copper, can be money. The Founding Fathers knew that the biggest enemy of sound money was government. They knew that inflation was a tool of government to steal from the masses. The new populist government violated the Constitution without even the pretense of a legal argument, and substituted their own wisdom over that of the Founding Fathers.

The Rise of Populism

During the time of the gold standard consumer prices only varied up or down by about 2 percent. An ounce of gold bought about the same amount of goods and services year in and year out. That didn't mean that we didn't have panics or recessions—we did. But they were short-lived and things returned to normal quickly. Then, in 1909, the United States experienced a rather severe banking crisis. Major banks went under and depositors lost their savings. In an attempt to help, the populist movement, which was sweeping the country at that time, won the day and encouraged the government to create a central bank as a lender of last resort to back up banks that faced failure and closure. More importantly, it also gave the Fed the authority to create and regulate paper money and credit, and consequently to influence interest rates.

No longer was the market to be trusted with money and credit creation—the government was. Instead of the supply of money being limited to the production of metals, which was limited by nature, the government would simply print up paper dollars as needed. They could progressively increase the money supply in order to keep interest rates artificially low and foster what they thought could be permanent economic growth. They theorized that the only reason for recessions was the absence of money and credit as a stimulus. Tight money was the cause of recessions—easy money the cause of prosperity, they reasoned. The result was the Roaring Twenties. All of a sudden America was on a binge they couldn't get off of.

By 1929 the binge turned into panic buying as the increased money found its way into the stock market. The worst thing a guy could be accused of was to not own stocks in the greatest stock market boom in American history. The Fed, fearing the boom was artificial and getting way out of hand, panicked and slammed on the monetary brakes. They decreased the money supply by one-third overnight. The result was the crash of 1929 and the Great Depression of the thirties. No one had ever seen anything like it. A massive deflation took hold, causing a crisis that lasted for over a decade.

In 1933 President Roosevelt declared a bank holiday, confiscated the peoples' gold in an attempt to replenish the Treasuries' coffers and save the nation's credit, then devalued the dollar, which immediately increased the price of imported goods to an already impoverished population. Dollars were no longer convertible into gold even though the Constitution declared that they must be. The revolution was complete. The U.S. monetary system had been converted from a gold standard to a fiat standard where the quantity of money, and therefore the value of money, was determined not by the free market but by fiat. That is government decree. Deflation had set in, the likes of which no one had ever seen before. Unemployment went to 34 percent. Homes were foreclosed on, credit vanished, and businesses went bankrupt. And this was all done in an attempt to help. As stated previously, at the end of the day, government intervened into the economy in order to insure prosperity and promote social justice and ended up doing neither. In fact, they did just the opposite.

During the thirties every trick in the book was tried in order to end the depression. Grand public works programs were instituted. Social welfare programs were established. Taxes were raised on the rich to pay for these new schemes and help the poor. Redistribution was the battle cry of the day. Farmers were paid to burn their crops and paid not to plant new ones in a futile attempt to raise prices. Then came protectionism and the trade wars to protect our markets. It was an orgy of government gone wild.

By 1938, almost a decade after the stock market crash and the initiation of an array of new government rescue programs, employment and the economy were no better off than they were before the help from government began. Nothing worked to revive the economy. After every populist program imaginable, the country was still buried under the worst deflationary depression known in all of modern-day history.

Meanwhile the Fed was printing up fresh dollars in an inane attempt to eliminate deflation and create higher prices. Again nothing worked. It took World War II to pull the nation out of the depression—every government economic program that was tried was worse than useless.

A World in Transition

After the war ended the economy started a comeback as soldiers trained in new skills returned home and began new productive careers. Once again the Fed struggled to know what the right amount of money in circulation should be. In the late forties inflation, a term the American people were not familiar with, became a problem. The average person on the street saw it as rising prices. But a handful of economists identified it for what it was—the Fed's creation of too many dollars. Easy money was condemned this time by a vigorous handful of economists, writers, and commentators.

The Fed started pulling in the reins. They learned their lesson when it came to slamming on the brakes as they did in 1929, so they adopted a gradualist policy. Slowly inflation declined. The result was the "Nifty Fifties." Inflation returned to a low and stable rate due to a moderate monetary policy, and the government slowly began to step out of the economy and become small again. As government became smaller and less intrusive the economy became bigger and the economy and stocks went into a bull market that lasted nearly two decades.

But government could not leave well enough alone. In the mid-sixties President Johnson launched his Great Society programs, designed to help Americans achieve a better and more secure life. This led to what these kinds of government policies always lead to—trouble. First, in 1968, when the government found they needed more money to pay for their new welfare programs they passed a law removing the silver from American coins. Silver dollars were outlawed, and silver was extracted from other coins and replaced with tin and lead. After that bit of theft, they increased the supply of paper dollars to pay for their new social programs. By 1970 the Fed started financing the Vietnam war by once again increasing the money supply. By 1973 oil had skyrocketed and the Fed, in an attempt to prevent the economy from going into a recession, monetized the oil rise. In other words, rather than allowing the price of oil to act as a tax that reduces consumption, it increased the money supply so everyone would have enough money to pay for higher gas prices. It was paper money on top of paper money on top of paper money. This simply led to higher and higher overall inflation.

One main reason that drove the Fed to inflate during the 1970s was the passage of the Humphrey-Hawkins Act by Congress. This legislation charged the Fed with a new task: to encourage economic growth, fight high unemployment, and try to prevent possible recession, while at the same time fighting inflation. The legislation accomplished just the opposite. A new phenomenon developed called stagflation.

As government grew bigger, instituting new programs to help the poor, tax the rich, and control and regulate business, the economy responded as it always had: Unemployment skyrocketed to above 10 percent; an out-of-control monetary policy led to 12 percent inflation rates; we had three recessions in 10 years; and the dollar dropped like a rock, which took interest rates to 21 percent. Meanwhile gold, which was set free from its Roosevelt peg of $35 an ounce in 1933, was made convertible for the first time in 30 years and soared to over $800, the equivalent of $2,200 in inflation-adjusted terms, thereby exposing government's inflationary games over the previous three decades.

In 1980 Ronald Reagan was voted in as president and he, together with the help of Paul Volcker and later Alan Greenspan, returned to sound money policies, which returned the rate of monetary growth to much lower levels. The Reagan administration reduced the size of government, reduced tax rates, deregulated, and opened up international trade. The rest is history. The result was a period of 25 years of low inflation and unprecedented prosperity with only three negative quarters of growth in all those years.

The one thing that history teaches us is that the mandate of the Fed to both fight inflation and economic recessions is impossible to achieve. The Fed cannot, and never could, control the economy. Presidents Wilson and Roosevelt proved that; the Soviet Union and Communist China proved that; and Johnson, Nixon, and Carter proved that. But the Fed can control inflation. They can keep the money supply low and stable. They can approximate the gold standard where gold generally enters the economy at a 2 to 3 percent rate over long periods of time.

Greenspan used to explain to Congress every time he was challenged to do something to foster economic growth that the best way the Fed had of dealing with a slowing economy and a rising unemployment rate was to reduce inflation, and keep it low and under control. It is interesting that during Volcker's and Greenspan's tenures as chairmen of the Fed, the price of gold averaged about $500 for about 20 years. As soon as Ben Bernanke was named as the prospective new Fed chairman, gold began its ascent and has not looked back since. Maybe gold was signaling us to beware, even back then, of a change in monetary policy. And, indeed, today, we have a Fed that is erratic. The Fed is once again struggling to determine the proper level of money supply and interest rates.

The Fed of the twenty-first century needs to change, but change for the better. We know the lessons of the past. We know what has worked and what has not. We know that the Fed can create deflation as they did in the 1930s and inflation as they did in the 1970s. To avoid going through that unnecessary and very unpleasant experience again, the Fed needs to do the following things.

The Fed of the Twenty-First Century

First, the Fed should set the money supply to increase at a low and stable rate permanently. The late Milton Friedman, the modern-day father of monetarism, said that the Federal Reserve Board could be replaced by a computer. Some argue that the money supply is irrelevant in today's global economy. If that's true then there is no reason *not* to fix the increase of money. You don't need 12 people sitting around a table arguing about it. Just set it and leave it alone! A steady 2 to 3 percent increase in the monetary base would be just fine. This means that there will be a little inflation and a little deflation from time to time. They need to let both occur—it's a natural result of sound money.

Next, don't set interest rates. Let the Fed funds rate float just like any other interest rate. Why argue about what an interest rate should be when the market is telling you every minute of the day? And if they can't do that, peg it to the one-month or three-month T-bill rate. That is a market-oriented short-term rate. At least the funds rate will be market determined and not set by arbitrary decree.

This means ending the dual, and impossible, mandate of Humphrey-Hawkins. It means ending the Fed's attempt to target growth, which they cannot do, and control inflation, something they can do. This requires that the Fed allow the economy to go into recessions from time to time if interest rates rise. There is nothing wrong with a recession any more than there is something wrong with winter. It just happens—and there is nothing government can do about it anyway. Recessions are like the weather and the change of seasons. No act of Congress will change them or stop them from occurring. The same is true with panics and crises. They come with the territory and that territory is freedom. Freedom requires both the freedom to succeed and the freedom to fail. This is how we learn. The recent assumption that the government should do something to prevent the economy from going into recession presupposes that they can. Neither the government nor the Fed has the power to achieve that goal. They can only make things worse by trying. The one thing they can do and should do is to get out of the way. Let the economy adjust naturally.

Finally, a twenty-first century Fed in these times, and given a fiat standard, must be a banker of last resort. The concept of a banker's banker was invented to shore up market failures and severe economic disruptions. I see nothing wrong with this idea in general. The Fed buying assets, or lending against assets, or guaranteeing assets at desperation prices, is fine as long as they do not create or prevent victims.

It is because no one else is willing to or rich enough to touch these risky assets that the Fed finds itself in a unique position. They are able to acquire assets at bargain basement prices. In most transactions of this kind in the past the government has made money. Taxpayers have in total, over many such rescues, not been affected. Today, if the government bought all of the bad mortgage paper outstanding at pennies on the dollar, then resold whatever paper was performing when markets were normal, the taxpayer would probably be the beneficiary. The Fed should be a last-resort buyer of assets only if and when necessary. If things become really dire, then the Fed is there to buy when there are no other buyers. They are there to make a market or clear a market when markets cannot do that for themselves. (To date, the government has made money on their purchases and loans.)

The standard by which government decides to intervene must always be the same: to prevent structural damage to the monetary and/or economic system. The line drawn between government intervention, regulation, and the sanctity of free markets is that such intervention must be to prevent fraud through regulation, through insuring transparency, and/or facilitate markets that are unable to function. It needs to provide transparency on such things as leverage and risk so that the markets can provide individuals with the information to judge such risk and take actions to protect themselves.

The Fed can assist in the orderly liquidation of large institutions in order to protect against economic contagion and structural damage. But this extraordinary intervention should always be a last resort. It should not be to prevent victims nor to create or protect new victims. The question of moral hazard needs to be answered by example. Every central bank action to preserve the system must result in those responsible or involved in such action ending up where they would have been without Fed intervention.

So, I'm not talking about a bailout; on the contrary. Companies, homeowners who can't make their mortgage payments, cities that have floated bad bonds, and financial institutions, creditors, and investors—all must be allowed to fail. The point is not to try and save a company or group of individuals. The point is to preserve the system and promote open and orderly markets. If successful the intervention of the central bank will have been neutral. There will be failures and victims specific to the institutions involved but without the spillover into the broad economy in general. This can prevent the onslaught of innocent victims who had nothing to do with the troubles of specific institutions. I see no sense in the Fed ever taking action or not taking action to try and solve a problem that would ultimately hurt the economy at large. Not when a surgical solution is possible.

But intervention should only be an option and never a mandate. Intervention during financial panics and crises is not always necessary and rarely the same. For example, the government let thousands of savings and loan banks go under in the 1980s without structural damage occurring. Hundreds more failed in the 1990s. These were controlled liquidations. The government guaranteed the savers' deposits, as promised. But the bankers and the banks themselves were allowed to fail. Another example is Long-Term Capital Management (LTCM), which was one of the largest financial institutions around. Then Fed Chairman Greenspan brought the interested creditors together and persuaded them to refinance the risky loans rather than "run" the bank. LTCM was saved and not a penny of taxpayer money was spent. More, the investors ended up making money rather than losing it. And although LTCM was liquidated two years later, it was orderly and there was no financial meltdown.

New York City was saved through government loans, as was Chrysler Corp. Both loans extended by the government were eventually paid back with interest. The government, therefore the American taxpayer, actually made money on the deal. Historically, the prices of these kinds of extraordinary interventions have been in their entirety low to taxpayers compared to the alternative and helped the market morph into a new less regulated financial industry over the years. The role of a modern-day central bank should amount to a stop-gap insurance program. Nothing more, nothing less. All the rest of its functions—money creation and the setting of interest rates—should be abandoned in favor of a market-oriented and automatic process. If we must be on a fiat standard, this is the best a fiat standard can be.

But, if you are going to have a fiat standard, it's going to come with more regulation than desired. That's the trade-off. A fiat standard requires more transparency, more monitoring, more regulation, and more taxpayer dollars to operate and support it than a gold standard. Fiat standards can work, but they are more costly and more intrusive than the automatic market process of the gold standard. The best a fiat standard can do is impersonate a gold standard. Such has been the case with the Fed regulating the money supply and interest rates rather than allowing the market to do it.

For my money and a host of other reasons, I'd prefer living under the gold standard any day. Perhaps we will some day, but until that day comes, the changes from the twentieth century Fed to the twenty-first century Fed are needed and needed now. This will bring us closer to the gold standard, which is still today an unknown ideal.

Much has been written and said of the Fed lately. Most of it is not flattering and belies the fact that if the gold standard was as flawed as its critics argue, certainly it can be argued that the present day fiat system has proven to be flawed as well. It is more closely watched than ever before. It is also more criticized today than in decades. And because of it we have an excellent chance of changing the nature of the Fed today. In doing so we can end up with a more reliable, less disruptive, and more market-oriented monetary policy than at any time in the last hundred years.

Such a change would be most welcome.

Part II

THE INTERNATIONAL GOLD STANDARD

Chapter 6

The Making of an International Monetary Crisis[*]

F or years the world has been plagued by continuing international monetary crises. Since 1944, the international monetary system has endured dollar shortages and dollar gluts; chronic deficits and chronic surpluses; perpetual parity disequilibria and currency realignments; disruptive "hot money" flights of capita; and numerous controls on the exchange of money and goods.

---

[*]This article was reprinted from *The Freeman*, published by The Foundation for Economic Education, in April of 1973. It remains as pertinent today as then.

In 1968 a two-tier gold market was established in the midst of a run on U.S. Treasury gold reserves. In 1971 the two-tier experiment failed in the face of new foreign government demands for dollar convertibility: The United States embargoed gold and allowed the dollar to seek its own level on the free market. In December of 1971, a new agreement was reached—the Smithsonian Agreement— which consisted of multilateral revaluations of most major foreign currencies and a de facto devaluation of the dollar. In 1972 the dollar was officially devalued yet remained nonconvertible into gold.

Meanwhile, only 14 months after the Smithsonian Agreement was reached, the dollar was brought under new selling pressure and was again forced to devalue (a total of almost 20 percent in under two years), and the free market price of gold soared to nearly $100 an ounce, making the official price and the two-tier system look embarrassingly unrealistic.

The most immediate and visible cause of the 1971 international monetary crisis can be traced directly to an excess supply of dollars, which accumulated in foreign central banks. These dollars, some $60 billion at the time, were at one time theoretically claims on U.S. gold. But over the years, U.S. gold reserves (then about $10 billion) became conspicuously inadequate to meet foreign demand for gold convertibility.

At present, the major problem confronting economic and monetary policy makers is: What is to be done with the continuous accumulation over the years of surplus dollars held by the central banks of the western world?

Policy makers have instituted one stop-gap measure after another in order to buy the time necessary to solve this problem and to reach agreement on long-term monetary reform. But before one can determine which reforms are necessary for a successful future monetary system, one must know what monetary policies caused the past system to fail.

Today's policy makers have refused to identify the most fundamental cause of the international monetary crisis; they have never wanted to know which monetary theories and policies led to the excessive and disruptive amounts of dollars that now flood the world, for the answer is: their own monetary theories and domestic policies of artificial money and credit expansion. If one wishes to project the kinds of policies that will be employed internationally and the effects they will produce in the future, one need only to look at the monetary theories held by today's policy makers and their effects when implemented in the past.

Monetary Theory: Past

During the nineteenth century the free world was on what was called the classical gold standard. It was a period of unprecedented production. More wealth and a greater standard of living was achieved and enjoyed by more people than in all the previous history of the world. The two conditions most responsible for the great increase in wealth during the nineteenth century were free market capitalism and the gold standard: Capitalism because it provided a social system where individuals were free to produce and own the results of their labor; the gold standard because it provided a monetary system by which individuals could more readily exchange and save the results of their labor.

While capitalism afforded individuals the opportunity to trade in the open market, which led to economic prosperity, the gold standard provided a market-originated medium of exchange and means of saving, which led to monetary stability.

But because neither capitalism nor the gold standard were ever fully understood or consistently practiced, there existed a paradox during the nineteenth century: a series of disruptive economic and monetary crises in the midst of a century of prosperity.

No Curb on Governments

The world never achieved a pure gold standard. While individuals operated under a classical gold standard with the conviction that production was the only way to gain wealth, they allowed their government to become the exception to this rule.

Government produces nothing. During the nineteenth century it operated mostly on money it taxed from its citizens. As government's role increased, so did its need for money.

The policy makers knew that gold stood in the way of government spending and that direct confiscation of wealth via taxation was unpopular. So policy makers advocated a way of indirectly taxing productive people in order to finance both government programs and the increasing government bureaucracy necessary to implement those programs.

The method was to increase the money supply. Since government officials were not about to go out and mine gold, they had to rely on an artificial increase. Although the methods of artificial monetary expansion varied, the net effect remained the same: an increase in the claims to goods in circulation and a general rise in the prices of goods and services. The layman called this phenomenon "inflation." This invariably resulted in monetary crises and economic recessions.

Capitalism and gold got the blame for these crises, but the blame was undeserved.

Why then were capitalism and the gold standard not exonerated from this unearned guilt? Why were these two great institutions tried and sentenced to death by the slow strangulation of government laws? The verdict must read: "Found guilty due to inadequate defense."

The few whispers of defense from a handful of scholars were easily drowned out by every politician who argued for more government controls and regulations over the economy; by every professor who argued for the redistribution of private wealth and for government to provide for the welfare of some group at the expense of another; by every business person and his or her lobbyist who argued for government to subsidize their business or industry while protecting them from foreign competitors; by every economist who advocated that government should stimulate the economy; and by every media spokesperson who argued that the public should vote for policies of government intervention. These, and people like them, made up an army of educators.

The Policy Makers

They were the intellectuals who promoted theories that could not exist without the governmental expropriation of private funds; who sponsored, advocated, or encouraged government policies that would victimize individuals (taxation), deceive and defraud individuals (inflation), and turn individuals against one another (the redistribution of private wealth). They were the people who provided government with the theoretical ammunition necessary to disarm individuals of their rights. They educated the public on the blessings of government intervention, and they were the ones directly or indirectly responsible for all the subsequent coercive government actions and all of their economically disruptive effects.

59

They were (and still are) the policy makers. Policy makers damned capitalism and the gold standard as being inherently unstable. They attributed capitalism's productive booms to government's intervention into the economy, and the government-made busts to the gold standard and the greed of individuals.

Such distortions of truth could not be sold to the public easily. A united attack on common sense was necessary in order to obscure the virtues of freedom and the meaning of money.

The Process of Confusion

The policy makers led that attack. Armed with the slogans of a con man, they slowly obscured the obvious and concealed the sensible, cloaking monetary and economic theories in graphs, charts, and statistics, until people doubted their own ability to deal with the now esoteric problems of economy and state.

But the American public had great confidence in the integrity of their public leaders and trusted the knowledge of experts in the fields of higher learning, and so they accepted the conclusions of their policy makers.

The policy makers had made their first and most important move toward institutionalizing government intervention and their theories of artificial monetary expansion into the American way of life: they convinced the American public that individuals needed government protection from the natural recessions of capitalism and the monetary crises inherent in the gold standard.

Policy makers had to do a lot of talking to convince individuals that the most productive system ever known was the cause of recessions. They had to do even more talking to convince individuals that the precious metal freely chosen and held as money was the cause of monetary depreciation and the source of bank insolvency. It took a lot of talking, but when they had finished, they were convinced. They were convinced that their minds—their own eyes—had been deceiving them. They were convinced that the way to freedom was through greater controls and more restrictions, and that paper was as good as gold.

While the attack on capitalism was subtle and implicit, condemnation of the gold standard was open and explicit.

Condemnation of Gold

The reason for the policy maker's condemnation is that, even though governments never really adhered to it, the gold standard placed limits on the amount of artificial money and credit a government could create. Money and credit expansion were always brought to a quick end because banks and governments had to redeem their notes in gold. Redemption was the major obstacle in the way of the policy makers' dream of unlimited artificial money creation and unlimited spending.

The policy makers learned how to obtain in a matter of minutes the purchasing power of 50 productive individuals working 50 weeks. They learned of the plunder and loot that a button on a printing press would provide. But it would not be until the twentieth century that they would convince the government to eliminate gold and convince people of the virtues of legal counterfeiting. The policy makers had to destroy an individual's idea of property in order to entice people with dreams of unearned wealth. The policy makers had to persuade them of the "merits" of monetary redistribution and government handouts.

If there was a monetary rule of conduct among individuals during the days of the semi-gold standard it was: the person who desires to gain wealth must earn it, by producing goods or their equivalent in gold. It was in this spirit and by this golden rule of conduct that individuals could and did operate in the monetary and economic spheres of society. Consequently, they achieved the most productive and beneficial era that mankind had ever known.

But what they never identified or challenged was the opposing monetary rule of conduct advocated by their policy makers: the government that aims to acquire wealth must confiscate it—or counterfeit its equivalent in paper claims.

Evolution of the Theory

The gold standard limited artificial monetary expansion and in doing so, it limited artificial economic expansion. The policy makers considered this great virtue of the gold standard to be its major vice.

The policy makers saw that artificial monetary expansion had led to economic booms. They also saw that at the end of every artificial boom there occurred a financial panic and recession.

The policy makers ignored the cause of financial panics; they saw only their effects—bank runs and the demand for gold redemption. They ignored the cause of economic recessions; they saw only that the boom had ended. Reversing cause and effect, the policy makers concluded: Eliminate gold redemption and the financial panics would stop; eliminate the gold standard and the boom would never end.

The policy makers had to make another major move toward institutionalizing government intervention and their theories of artificial monetary expansion into the American way of life: They had to divorce the idea of national production from the idea of individual productivity.

Ignoring the fact that the individual was the source of production, they convinced individuals that in the name of social prosperity, government could and should stimulate the economy and encourage national production; while at the same time they advocated income taxation to penalize individuals for being productive. Implicit in this doctrine is the idea that production is a gift of state, the result of government guidance; that individual productivity and accumulation of wealth is a sin, the result of human greed.

Individuals were subtly offered a false alternative: the permission to produce and be taxed directly through government confiscation or the luxury of an artificial boom, to be taxed indirectly through inflation.

The American people rejected both alternatives (and still do today) yet saw no other acceptable course of action—the intellectual opposition was still too weak to provide them with one. Thus, by default, they accepted both alternatives to a limited degree. An income tax should be levied only on those who could afford it, while the government should steer the economy on a prosperous course.

How was the economy to be steered? By supplying unending paper reserves to a regimented banking system and compelling bankers to keep interest rates artificially low. In 1913 it was too early to sell the public on the virtues of the direct confiscation of gold. But the time was right for the takeover of the banking system. A monetary revolution was in store for America.

Fractional Reserve Banking

In the name of economizing gold (which allegedly was not in sufficient supply to be used as money), policy makers advocated a fractional reserve system. A fractional reserve system would by law set a ratio at which gold must be held to back legal tender notes. While fractional reserve banking had always been practiced by banks and condoned by governments, the policy makers formalized and legitimized it through the creation of the Fed domestically and the gold exchange standard internationally.

What the Fed and the gold exchange standard had in common was a central banking system that used as reserves both gold and money substitutes (such as demand deposits, fractionally backed Fed notes, and government securities backed by the taxing power of the government). These reserves—gold and the money substitutes—served as a base for monetary expansion. Gold was no longer the sole reserve asset: it was now supplemented by paper reserves. The government exercising a monopoly on the issuance of paper money could designate what should comprise the monetary reserves. Hence, redemption was now not only in gold, but also in money substitutes. In this way a pyramiding of money and credit expansion could take place without the automatic limitations imposed by the gold standard.

By the 1920s the Fed had grown and increased its power and controls, which enabled it to increase the money supply and reduce interest rates for longer periods of time. The Fed Board succeeded in implementing its easy money policies. The problem now was that money and credit became so easy to obtain that it spilled over into the stock market and other investment areas. Leverage through the use of margin sent stocks soaring.

The government became alarmed over this wild speculation, raised interest rates and margin requirements sharply, and slammed on the monetary brakes—but it was too late. The day came (that inevitable day) in October 1929 when the Law of Causality presented its bill.

Investors found that their profits were merely paper profits, that their prosperity was an illusion. The stock market crashed.

Individuals suddenly realized that on the other side of the coin of credit there existed debt. Industries fought to become liquid; everyone tried to get hard cash. But the hard cash—the gold—was insufficient to cover the outstanding claims.

The Great Depression

The policy makers succeeded in implementing their theories, yet all of the consequences that their theories were to have eliminated confronted them once again—this time to a far greater degree. This was the Great Depression; this was the monetary crisis that not only forced an entire national banking system to close its doors but was of international dimensions. The dollar was in trouble not only at home but also abroad. What to do?

The policy makers had the answer. They viciously condemned gold and capitalism for causing the crisis and advocated even greater policies of money and credit expansion in order to stimulate the economy; more government controls, more government regulations, more and higher taxes were the answer. People were asked to patriotically give up their gold in order to save the nation's credit. It was a time of emergency, so Americans complied. They did not know that they would never see their gold again, that taxes would continue to rise higher and higher, and that inflation would become a way of life.

The policy makers had to do a lot of talking to convince individuals of the evils of gold and capitalism. They had to do a lot of talking, but when they were finished, people were convinced. They were convinced that nothing less than the direct confiscation of wealth and a vigorous credit expansion could save the nation.

Devaluation in 1934

In 1934, with one stroke of a pen, Franklin D. Roosevelt confiscated the entire gold stock of America. When government held the gold and the citizens held only paper, the government reduced the value of their paper by over 40 percent, raising the official dollar price of its gold holdings. (The policy makers had learned that credit expansion meant debt creation but showed governments how to default on their debts by devaluing the monetary unit in relation to gold and other currencies.)

The United States was now on a fiat standard domestically, and again in the name of economizing gold, the government printed new money against its total stock of newly acquired gold. Deficit spending became a way of life and government borrowing became so insatiable that any mention of paying off the national debt was smeared as unrealistic and regressive in light of the virtues of continued monetary expansion. (The policy makers had learned that borrowing meant debt accumulation but showed the government how to amortize its debts by charging its citizens through higher interest rates and direct and hidden taxes.)

Domestically the fiat standard has failed miserably. It was designed to economize gold and provide a stable dollar. Since 1913, the dollar has lost most of its purchasing power. The fractional gold cover has been progressively reduced and transferred to cover obligations abroad. That gold reserve has been reduced through demands for redemption by foreign governments that finally forced the United States to close the doors of its central bank. (The central bank was supposed to be a bank of last resort. The run on the Treasury's gold amounted to the largest and most prolonged bank run in the history of any nation.)

Bretton Woods

Meanwhile, internationally, in 1944 a new system was established—the Bretton Woods system. During the Bretton Woods era, policy makers adopted policies of vigorous credit expansion as a panacea for the world's problems. The instrument of credit used was the dollar. In its role as reserve currency, the dollar was considered "as good as gold" and served as a supplement to world gold reserves. In the name of world liquidity, dollars would be furnished as needed to replenish and build up war-torn nations and world reserves. The dollar was envisioned as a stable yet ever-expanding reserve currency.

In this spirit, dollars poured forth on demand via U.S. deficits in the form of foreign aid, loans, and military expenditures. Foreign demand for dollars never ceased, nor did the expansion of money and credit, until the world found itself in the midst of an inflationary spiral that turned to recession and ended in an international monetary crisis: the dollar inconvertible, dropping in value, an undesirable credit instrument and ineffective reserve currency.

The dollar was again devalued, while gold soared in value, reaching new highs. And through all this, policy makers have been screaming the same old theories: "Gold is a barbarous relic! It ought to be eliminated completely! What we need is more liquidity . . . more money and credit!"

What more can the policy makers do?

The Theory Projected

There is a causal link between history and future events. A theory is a policy or set of ideas proposed as the basis for human action. To the extent that a theory furthers individuals' lives it is practical and therefore a good theory. To the extent that a theory destroys individuals' lives it is impractical, self-defeating, and therefore a bad theory.

A sound monetary theory, if employed, will facilitate trade and economic growth, while an unsound monetary theory will lead to monetary crises and economic disruptions.

The policy makers have been charged with providing theoretical ammunition to government. To the policy makers' great discredit they have learned nothing about monetary theory in the last two centuries, save how to employ more sophisticated techniques of credit expansion. They have rejected the lessons of history through self-induced blindness and have made themselves deaf and dumb to rational economic analysis. They see nothing except their precious theories of artificial monetary expansion.

Today's policy makers see themselves as participating in an evolution of the international monetary system comparable in "importance" to the role their intellectual ancestor played in evolving the gold standard into the gold exchange standard and the gold exchange standard into the Bretton Woods system. And if by "evolution" the policy makers mean a series of changes in a given direction, this is a correct description of their role. But it is the wrong direction. And it has been the wrong direction for over a century.

Given the monetary theories held by today's policy makers who are concerned with international monetary reform, one can expect a change only in the method and degree of monetary expansion—not a change in direction.

Each time the policy makers have seen their monetary theories implemented they have blinded themselves to their effects. Each time a monetary or economic crisis has occurred they have refused to identify the cause. The cause can usually be identified easily by looking for government intervention into the economy: providing newly printed money and credit that causes inflation, malinvestment, over-consumption, the misallocation of resources—distortions and mistakes that, when liquidated, are called recessions. If economic history has tended to repeat itself, it is because the policy makers have been guiding human action and government policies along a circular theoretical course that has been tried and has failed—again and again and again.

"If at First You Don't Succeed . . ."

The spectacle of billions of inconvertible dollars frozen in the vaults of central banks has brought on cries of condemnation over the dollar's credibility as a reserve currency. The policy makers' theory of a stable yet artificially ever-expanding reserve currency has failed.

The solution to the problem (if the policy makers are to remain consistent) will be to evolve the international monetary system from a system in which an ever-expanding reserve currency provided the world with credit and liquidity to a system in which an ever-expanding reserve asset will fill that role. Like the dollar, this reserve asset will amount to circulating debt, that is something owed rather than something owned. It will be a nonmarket instrument, deriving its acceptability from government cooperation and decree, immune from the laws of the free market and outside the reach of greedy speculators.

Where will this asset come from? Under the Bretton Woods system, dollar reserves were furnished by the U.S. central bank. Both the bank and the asset failed to provide sufficient stability. The next step is to create a world bank (a larger bank of last resort) controlled by an international organization, the International

Monetary Fund (IMF), with the power to create a new asset, independent of any single government's monetary policy.

As a supplement to gold and like the dollar before it, this asset should be a credit instrument. Unlike the dollar, it would have the backing of an entire world of central banks. The asset should be ever-expanding and should provide both liquidity and stability. In short, it should be as good as gold.

The SDR: As Good as Gold Again!

Special Drawing Rights (SDRs) or "paper gold," as those who can keep a straight face sometimes refer to it, was introduced to the international monetary system in 1967. It was a time when the dollar was under suspicion and gold was increasingly demanded.

In order to economize gold, the IMF issued a new reserve asset (SDRs) to supplement gold and take pressure off the dollar. The SDR is a bookkeeping entry, defined in gold yet nonconvertible into gold. It serves the same function as gold since it is a reserve, but unlike gold, it can be created by a stroke of the pen.

Policy makers have chosen the SDR as the reserve asset most likely to succeed in replacing gold and the dollar. But just as the dollar was supposed to be as good as gold and was not, the SDR, even if made tangible and convertible into gold and/or other currencies, will suffer the same demise.

The policy makers have chosen to ignore the fact that there is no fundamental difference between an artificially ever-expanding reserve currency and an artificially ever-expanding reserve asset—both are inflationary and therefore self-destructive.

But the real threat is not that the SDR may fail as the dollar did in bringing monetary stability. The threat is in the damage SDRs can do if developed within a formal system. Just as the dollar replaced gold as the primary asset, SDRs have a very real potential for further diminishing both the role of gold and the dollar, and in doing so changing the entire nature and inflationary potential of the IMF.

Debt Amortization or Default: The False Alternative

Basically, monetary reform boils down to the following two alternatives: Some countries advocate defaulting on foreign debts via devaluation, some countries advocate creating more foreign debts via artificial reserve expansion, SDRs. The kind of debt creation that is consistent with the policy makers' theories amounts to a method of constantly refinancing government debt below the market rate of interest. Given the past record of government, the principal may never be repaid in full or in real money terms, so debt creation actually amounts to slow and less visible, but inevitable, debt default.

A third alternative is simply to not create debts that governments are unable or unwilling to repay. The third alternative is for governments to stop arbitrarily creating debt instruments such as the dollar in its role as reserve currency and the SDR. These instruments and the currencies printed against them invariably depreciate and cause monetary crises. The third alternative would mean returning to the gold standard, which limits credit and monetary creation, and which, in today's enlightened era and within our evolving economic structure, is considered passé and old-fashioned.

Thus, in the present political context, monetary reform will consist of devaluation and the default on debts, or artificial reserve expansion and the amortization of debts, or, more probably, a combination of both.

What is the difference between default and amortization?

Consider the example of people whose expenditures have for some time been exceeding their income. They are, in effect, running a deficit. They find themselves with more short-term claims against themselves than they have liquid assets. If they refuse to liquidate assets and find a way to default on their short-term claims, the loss falls directly on their creditors. (When governments default on their creditors, they call it devaluation.)

But what if these people refinance their short-term obligations by printing longer-term IOUs and offer interest on this newly created note? What if this new note is then used as an asset by creditors who, in turn, print IOUs against it and distribute these as direct claims to goods, in effect turning them back into money? Here the loss falls on all those who are in the domain of the counterfeiters and who must suffer the effects of artificially rising prices.

From this example, the following conclusion can be drawn relative to governments: any form of debt default falls squarely on the shoulders of the creditors, that is, on the citizens of creditor governments. Any form of debt amortization, however, falls indiscriminately on the shoulders of all those individuals within the monetary sphere of those governments participating in an international monetary system of debt creation. No ring of international counterfeiters has ever been, or could ever be, more of a threat to individuals and their wealth than is the IMF in its move toward international monetary reform.

The Frightening Prospect of an International Debt

In the past, devaluation and default on excessive debt has been the method most used to eliminate debt. But, given an international system of artificial reserve expansion, the issuance of credit and the amortization of debts may be expected to give rise to the specter of an international debt.

The possibility of an international debt is not a pleasant one to contemplate, like a national debt that continues to grow without restraint through continuous refinancing; an international debt would soon become uncontrollable and self-perpetuating.

The victims of such debt creation must ultimately be individuals: taxpayers to the degree the debt is financed directly or repaid; consumers to the degree that the debt is financed indirectly through the inflationary method of money creation; or creditors if and when (or to the degree that) the debt is ultimately repudiated.

Given the choice of amortization and default as methods of dealing with the problem of debt, and given the inflationary policies that governments are determined to follow, it makes little difference what kind of monetary reform is implemented. Our monetary authorities are only haggling over who should be the victims of their debt creation—foreigners or nationals.

Rational and morally concerned individuals will not cheer their government for shifting the burden of their debt onto foreign citizens through the process of debt default and devaluation. On the other hand, given greater and greater debt creation, the citizens of all countries will suffer the inevitable result of more taxation and more inflation.

Thus an individual will pay taxes, and on top of that the hidden tax of inflation, for domestic programs, and on top of that an inflationary tax for world expenditures, and on top of that the inflationary tax for interest on all inflationary debts both domestic and international.

Toward an International Fiat Reserve System

It is not an easy thing to eliminate gold from a monetary system and replace it with the continuously depreciating promises of paper money and paper assets. All such money substitutes at one time derived their value from and were dependent on the real values of commodities. It takes a lot of time and a lot of talking to convince individuals to accept artificial values based on political paper promises. In America, policy makers have had a century in which to propagate their monetary theories and institutionalize them within the policies of state. The result has been the slow erosion and obscuring of gold's role in the monetary systems of humanity.

The monetary system that lies at the end of the policy makers' theories is an international fiat reserve system. The foot in the door that opens the way to this system is the SDR. Given the theories of world policy makers, the most probable proposal would be for the IMF to issue SDRs backed by a fractional amount of gold, dollars, or a basket of currencies or commodities. The effect of such a policy would be to cede to the IMF the power to create reserves out of thin air and set in motion the unrestricted workings of an international fractional reserve system.

A sequence of events typical of what one might expect from policy makers would be for them to advocate the establishment of a central bank (the IMF) that has the power to create reserve assets, define the asset in gold to give it credibility (fractionally backing the asset with a percentage of gold to give it further credibility), and, in the name of economizing gold, increase SDR allotments based on, and tied to, a basket of currencies and/or commodities, thereby reducing and eventually eliminating the gold backing, thus facilitating the constant increase in fiat reserves.

Ultimately this system would eliminate any objective limitations on monetary expansion, thereby surrendering monetary policy into the collective hands of a world body, the monetary heads of which would subjectively decide which nations will be given the special right to consume goods and at whose expense.

Simply Repetitious

This is not a prediction of coming events. It is simply an example of the methods policy makers would most likely advocate to achieve their objectives. (Currently, the IMF is contemplating issuing two trillion dollars in SDRs.) Notice that there is nothing particularly innovative about creating a fiat instrument, arbitrarily decreeing its value by deceit and force, then proceeding through fractional reserve banking and monetary expansion to systematically undermine the acceptability it had enjoyed by reason of its gold backing. It has all been done before.

These people are not innovators. They are simply repetitious! They would be laughable if they weren't so dangerous. But today's policy makers are dangerous. They have the power of government force in back of all the theories they propagate. And at the end of their theories awaits chaos. Given today's context, an international fiat reserve system must ultimately add to massive inflation as governments are inclined to spend more and more. This must lead to the eventual collapse of the international monetary system and with it the economies of the world.

The Real Meaning of Monetary Reform

Monetary crises are not born from nature, they are made—man-made.

As long as governments continue to adopt policies of inflationary finance, the monetary systems of finance will be in perpetual disintegration. This disintegration will lead to crises of greater scope and intensity, recurring at shorter intervals, while the meetings on monetary reform become a way of life as policy makers offer only variations of their destructive and futile theories.

As long as governments continue their policies of artificial monetary expansion there can be no such thing as monetary reform. To reform means to abandon those policies that have proven to be unjust and incorrect. Fundamental monetary reform means that governments would have to abandon their policies of inflationary finance.

The essence of contemporary monetary policy is the employment of inflationary finance, which means injustice to individuals that must bear the brunt of the amortization and default of government debt and the continuous depreciation in the value of their currencies. Further, it means that individuals will be forced to suffer the unnecessary and harmful effects of continuous recessions and inflation.

Until fundamental reform is achieved, the individual will remain the source of government financing. One can easily see that the source is being more and more exploited as governments resort to greater and more extensive policies of monetary expansion.

If fundamental reform does not occur, it is only a matter of time until private property is squandered in an inflationary system of waste. In the last analysis, real monetary reform must consist of returning to a gold standard. But there are preconditions that must be met before a gold standard can be established as a lasting monetary system.

Individuals must understand what money is. They must rediscover why gold is the most effective medium of exchange and means of saving. And individuals must discover what money is not. They must understand that by accepting a monetary unit by decree, they are not only condoning theft but are sanctioning the instrument of their own monetary and economic destruction. When individuals have understood this they will want to return to the gold standard.

But the gold standard cannot survive in an economy mixed with socialist controls and vaguely defined freedoms. Individuals must rediscover the virtues of the gold standard; they will not rediscover the virtues of the gold standard until they rediscover the virtues of capitalism. They will not rediscover the virtue of capitalism until they identify the nature of individual rights, the injustices of the initiation of force, and the violation of property rights.

If the gold standard is to return to this country, it will return on the wings of capitalism and not before.

If one wishes to fight for economic and monetary stability, one must also fight for capitalism. If one wishes to fight for capitalism, one must fight for individual rights. If one wishes to engage in this fight, the battle lines are clear: one must engage in an intellectual battle to end the theories held by their intellectual adversaries— the advocates of policies based on force, deceit, and fraud.

Chapter 7

The Death of Bretton Woods: A History Lesson*

I n 1944, as the world was recovering from the effects of World War II, the heads of state from over 100 countries met in Bretton Woods to create an international monetary system that would unite the western world, insure monetary stability, and facilitate international trade. Since then the system has been plagued

---

*This article was also first published in *The Freeman*, May 1973, by the Foundation for Economic Education. It is, once again, as pertinent in today's world as it was then. Some things never change.

by dollar shortages and dollar gluts, chronic deficits and chronic surpluses, perpetual parity disequilibria, "hot money" capital flows, and currency depreciation. By 1968 a two-tier gold market was established in the midst of a gold crisis that, by 1971, culminated in the suspension of dollar convertibility together with a dollar devaluation against multilateral revaluations of most other major foreign currencies.

Bretton Woods is dead and an autopsy is called for to determine the cause of death. If meaningful international monetary reform is to follow, it is necessary to know what went wrong.

Fixed Exchange Rates, Flexible Rules

Under the rules established by the Bretton Woods agreement, the gold values of a member nation's currency could be altered as conditions warranted. This distinguishing feature of the Bretton Woods system exposed a drastic ideological departure from the gold standard.

Under the gold standard, no natural conditions would ever warrant a change in the gold value of a nation's currency. Under a pure gold standard, all the money in circulation would be either gold or claims to gold. Any paper money would be fully convertible into gold. There would be no difference between claims to gold and gold itself, since, if claims to gold circulated as money, the gold could not.

However, there are government-made conditions that could warrant a reduction in the gold value of a nation's currency. If governments have the power to artificially increase the claims to gold (e.g., dollars), they have the power to depreciate the value of the national monetary unit.

Bretton Woods was established with the intention of aiding governments in exercising their powers of inflationary finance. Government leaders knew that the gold standard prevented them from fully pursuing domestic goals that depended on deficit spending and prolonged, artificially induced booms. They detested the gold standard for its fixed rules, which brought adverse economic repercussions whenever they refused to adhere to them, and they detested flexible exchange rates that exposed the government's policy of currency depreciation.

The political temptations of artificially increasing the money supply in order to stimulate the economy prevailed against the gold standard and brought the beginning of a new era: fixed exchange rates with flexible rules, the exact opposite of the gold standard.

No longer would politicians adhere to the discipline of the gold standard. No longer would they have to restrict their deficits or domestic money supplies. Government leaders would make their own rules and fix the nominal value of money by decree. And if conditions warranted a reduction in the nominal value of a nation's money, it was agreed that a nation could devalue up to 10 percent after the formality of obtaining other nations' permission. This was called the adjustable peg system.

The great ideological distinction between the gold standard and the Bretton Woods system, then, is that the Bretton Woods system was ostensibly intended to stabilize exchange rates, but at the same time it anticipated that governments would not defend the value of their currencies. Worse, Bretton Woods institutionalized a method that allowed and condoned future currency depreciation.

Export or Devalue: Institutionalizing the Devaluation Bias

Historically (and the Bretton Woods era was no exception) nations have seen fit to pursue a basically mercantilist trade policy; namely, a policy that maintains various regulations intended to produce more exports than imports.

The mercantilist case is not a realistic one. For example, it would be impossible to develop a logical case advocating that all individuals should sell products and services at the same time. Obviously, some individuals must be consumers if there is to be a market for sellers.

There is no difference when it comes to nations trading in a world market. This is simply to say that not all nations can run trade surpluses at the same time.

An equally difficult case would be to try to convince some individuals that most of the money they receive from the sale of goods and services should be saved rather than spent on the consumption of goods. Yet this is the intent underlying all government policies that aim at increasing exports (sales) and restricting imports (consumption).

There is no logical reason why individuals should not be allowed to reduce their cash balances by buying goods from other nations if they believe it is to their benefit; that is what their cash balances are for. To penalize people or discourage them from importing by imposing licensing restrictions, capital controls, tariffs, or import surcharges, only serves to limit the variety of their economic choices. This in turn only serves to reduce their standard of living. A nation's drive for export surpluses, together with its protectionist policies of restricting imports, leads to an increase in the domestic money supply. This influx of money, together with the money that governments feel they must artificially create in order to stimulate the economy, leads to higher domestic wages and prices as more money chases fewer goods. These higher wages and prices create an illusion of prosperity, which explains the popularity of mercantilist–inflationist policies.

But higher domestic wages and prices lead to a dwindling trade surplus as a nation's goods become less competitive in world markets and a dwindling trade surplus, unless corrected, eventually deteriorates into a trade deficit. This is the dilemma facing all governments that pursue the contradictory and self-defeating policies of mercantilism and inflationary finance.

Under a gold standard there are only two ways to resolve this dilemma: stop artificially creating money and stop preventing money from leaving the country. The result would be a normal, self-correcting deflation—a contraction of the domestic money supply—that would lead to a fall in domestic prices and to equilibrium in that nation's balance of trade-position.

But because governments hold an unwarranted fear of lower prices and favor higher prices that give the illusion of prosperity, the framers of Bretton Woods adopted a mechanism that would allow governments to inflate their currencies yet escape the process of a normal self-correcting deflation. By devaluing their currencies, governments could continue to inflate their domestic wages and prices while making their exports less expensive to the world.

The device of devaluation was established to allow nations to regain their competitive edge once their surplus deteriorated into deficit. Devaluation immediately lowers the price of a nation's exports, and in this way nations can more actively strive for export surpluses. Thus the framers of Bretton Woods found a way in which nations could continue both their drive for export surpluses and their domestic policies of inflation.

A nation would simply export its goods until its domestic inflation reduced or eliminated its trade surplus and then devalue. In this way the Bretton Woods system established an implicit code of conduct: export or devalue. It institutionalized a devaluation bias within the new international monetary system, which led to serious imbalances, ultimately resulting in hundreds of devaluations during the Bretton Woods era.

"Hot Money" Blues

Because devaluations are completely arbitrary (at best mere guesswork), new problems arose in place of old ones. The problems centered on the pre-devaluation exchange rate: nations were committed to supporting the rate even when it was unrealistic.

Bright investors soon began to realize when a particular currency was overvalued and to shift their money from the weak currency to stronger ones. This caused further pressure on exchange rates and resulted in speculation—selling short on X currency, buying gold, or going long on Y currency. Governments intervened in foreign exchange markets in order to preserve their unrealistic exchange rates by accumulating massive amounts of unwanted weak currencies. But this could not continue for long.

Finally, when a government was forced to devalue, the action had repercussions on other currencies (particularly if a major currency was involved): It brought all other weak currencies under suspicion. This resulted in further devaluations as investors transferred their money into only the strongest currencies in anticipation of competitive devaluations and major currency realignments. This was called "hot money" and was attributed to speculators—not to currency-depreciating policies of governments.

Finally, under the Bretton Woods agreement, national currencies were not allowed to float and seek their own levels. The IMF arbitrarily set the new par value of a currency—and this was consistently either too high or too low. Like all forms of government price-fixing, the fixed exchange rate system was in perpetual disintegration. This resulted in further "hot money" flurries, further realignments of currencies, and an inherently unstable exchange rate system—the exact opposite of the goal intended by the framers of monetary reform at Bretton Woods.

The Role of the Dollar under Bretton Woods

The role of the dollar under the Bretton Woods system was vastly different from that of other currencies. Because of the United States' economic strength and Europe's economic weakness after World War II, the dollar was used by other governments as a reserve for their currencies. This meant the dollar was pegged to gold and supposedly committed to stability and convertibility. Thus the dollar was supposed to be as good as gold and therefore to be treated as a reserve asset just like gold.

There are several implications tied to the concept of a paper reserve currency.

1. Gold, the main reserve asset, was considered too limited in quantity to restore world liquidity or to provide sufficient wealth for rebuilding war-torn nations.

2. While gold could not be increased, a paper asset (U.S. dollars) could—consequently the reserves of the western world could be expanded.

3. Inflation could be implemented in a more equitable manner by an ever-increasing paper reserve.

4. A paper reserve currency should not be devalued yet it should be increased as needed to meet demand. This last blatant contradiction was the major factor in the disintegration of the status quo international monetary system in later years.

Limited Gold—Unlimited Dollars: A Formula for Disaster

Since gold was limited, the vast majority of the assets on which foreign currencies were based to finance Europe's recovery were not gold but U.S. dollars—the second primary reserve asset. The demand for dollars came in two forms: (1) demand for foreign exchange to be used for importing goods and (2) demand for reserve liquidity and replenishment.

The United States satisfied the demand for foreign exchange by inflating its currency and extending loans and gifts to Europe. These gifts and loans were used almost entirely to import goods from the United States. Therefore, many of these dollars returned to the United States. However, the demand for reserve liquidity and replenishment was met by continuing U.S. deficits that led to European stockpiling of dollars in the form of interest-bearing notes and demand deposit accounts. Demand for dollars between 1950 and 1957 continued and an excess of dollars began to build up in foreign central banks.

After 1957, and to this day, the foreign banks have been obliged to continue to take in dollars that were neither intended for imports nor needed for liquidity. This era has become known as the era of the dollar glut.

Confidence versus Liquidity—A Two-Tier Tale

During the 1960s the progressive supply and accumulation of dollars mounted and world central bankers found themselves confronted with a government-made monetary dilemma: the more dollar reserves they acquired, the more likely was the chance that their dollar surplus would depreciate in value. To state the problem another way, the more liquidity central bankers enjoyed, the less confidence they had in their most liquid asset—the dollar.

Gresham's Law prevailed and in 1968 central bankers and private speculators began to convert their dollars into gold. A gold crisis developed: The United States could not hope to convert the amount of dollars outstanding against its gold stock. A two-tier gold market was set up to avert a dollar devaluation and the breakup of the International Monetary Fund, that is, one free market for speculators and industrial users who would buy gold at the free market price, and an official market where governments would transact dealings at the pegged price of $35 per ounce. Finally in 1971, in a wave of "hot money" speculation, the United States was forced to devalue the dollar against gold and to suspend its convertibility.

Gold's Limitations: A Blessing in Disguise

The demise of Bretton Woods can be traced directly to an excessive supply of dollars. The anti-gold principles of inflationary finance practiced diligently under the Bretton Woods era, turned into a give-and-take fiasco: The United States became a faucet of wealth, supplying dollars on request to every corner of the world, while over a hundred countries drained the United States in the name of world liquidity and reparations.

The result was a flood of dollars that swept over the world, producing world inflation, numerous recessions, hundreds of currency realignments, disruptive trade, a gold crisis, and the final international monetary crisis that has left the world precariously groping for stop-gap measures to resume monetary and trade transactions.

Clearly the Bretton Woods vision of a stable and ever-expanding reserve currency was doomed from the onset. Had the governments limited their reserves to gold, the kind of monetary and credit expansion under Bretton Woods—and all of its disastrous consequences—could never have occurred. Gold places objective limits on monetary and credit expansion, and this in itself was enough for the framers of Bretton Woods to condemn it.

It is no accident that the kind of limitations gold imposes on the extension of money, credit, and reserves is just what the world is crying for today in light of the dollar glut. As a reserve currency, the dollar was supposed to be as good as gold. But monetary authorities never stopped to ask, "What makes gold so good?" The answer is that gold is limited—the very point for which it was condemned.

The refusal of government leaders to adhere to the rules of the gold standard and their desire to create a monetary system based on their own arbitrary rules of whim and decree, failed as it has always failed. Once again, history has proved that a mixture of government whim with the laws of economics is not a prescription to cure world problems: It has always been and will always be a formula for world chaos.

U.S. Balance of Payments Problems

U.S. balance of payments deficits began in the early 1950s and have not ceased to this day. The cause of these incessant deficits can be traced to monetary and trade decisions made at the inception of Bretton Woods and reinforced throughout its existence.

The First Straw When it was decided that the United States was to act as world banker and benefactor to those countries in need of help after World War II, it is doubtful that anyone really believed the United States would profit as world banker. On the contrary, the consensus was that war-torn nations needed more money than they could afford to pay back. It was argued that the United States could afford to (and therefore should) extend foreign aid (gifts), loans at below market rates of interest (gifts), and military protection (gifts), to those countries in need.

What must be remembered is the precedent for this decision: the United States was committed to protect and finance the western world by virtue of its great strength and an ever-expanding stream of dollars.

It was assumed that this money would return to the United States via import demand and, in fact, during the years 1946 to 1949 most of it did, resulting in fantastic U.S. surpluses.

On Selling One's Cake and Wanting It Too But during the years 1950 to 1957 a turn of events took place. Europe, by design, curtailed its already abundant imports and concentrated on replenishing its national reserves. With conscious intent, the United States continued to supply the world with dollars through deliberate balance of payments deficits to accommodate Europe's demand for reserve replenishment. The refusal of foreign governments to allow their citizens to use their constantly rising dollar surpluses for U.S. goods (by imposing trade restrictions) led to the dollar glut of the 1960s.

The blame for the chronic surpluses of foreign governments and chronic deficits of the United States must be shared. While the United States can be blamed for financial irresponsibility, the surplus countries must be blamed for economic irresponsibility. The United States could have stopped its deficits, but surplus-ridden countries could have stopped penalizing their citizens and discouraging them from importing. Instead, they decided to increase dollar reserves (dollars that for the most part were given or loaned to them) and to either exchange them for gold or hold them in the form of interest-bearing notes and accounts.

By accumulating excessive amounts of dollars that they refused to use, surplus countries helped foster U.S. deficits: Some nations' chronic surpluses must mean that other nations are running deficits. The irony of the decision to run an intentional chronic surplus is that the purpose of selling goods is to gain satisfaction as an eventual consumer. The drive for both surplus reserves and surplus exports, and the refusal to consume goods with the money received, implies that a nation expects to sell a good and somehow derive satisfaction from it after it's gone.

The Illusion of the Last Straw   The increasing demand for dollars led the U.S. government and the Fed to increase the amount of dollars, thereby depreciating the purchasing power of the dollar. As confidence disappeared in the dollar's ability to continue its role as a reserve currency, "hot money" flurries soon appeared. Thus, by the late 1960s and early 1970s, an enormous amount of dollars accumulated against a dwindling supply of U.S. gold. This caused both runs on the U.S. gold stock and flights from the dollar into stronger or undervalued currencies.

This speculative capital outflow caused the U.S. balance of payments deficit to increase in a pyramiding fashion. Finally, the conspicuously low amount of U.S. gold reserves, the disparity between currencies and interest rates, and a deteriorating balance of payments aroused a well-founded suspicion that the dollar might be devalued—and that other, stronger currencies might appreciate in value.

This justifiable suspicion then caused even greater U.S. capital outflows, which led to even greater U.S. deficits. This was the straw that broke the camel's back. But it was the haystack of straws before it, beginning with the first straw—the first U.S. inflation-financed gift abroad—that inexorably led to the progression of U.S. balance of payments deficits, international monetary chaos, and the disintegration of the Bretton Woods system.

The High Price of Gifts When the United States embarked on a policy of inflation-financed world loans and gifts, it surrendered all hopes of attaining balance of payments equilibrium for itself or for the world. Between the years 1946 and 1969, the United States, as world banker, extended some $83 billion in grants and loans. Since 1958 some $95 billion has left the country. Most of these dollars were nonmarket transactions motivated by political and military considerations.

While many economists believe it is necessary for the United States to run trade surpluses to correct its balance of payments deficits, to expect normal exports to rise to the level of these abnormal capital outflows only makes sense if one stands on one's head—it is not a logical position to take.

These grants should never have been given to foreign nations. It was an economically unsound move and the grants were extended at the expense of the American taxpayers. Further, any additional loans and gifts made by the United States to satisfy nations who demand free military protection, such as Europe and Japan, will only lead to further capital outflows, and this at a time when the world is plagued by depreciating dollar reserves and continuing U.S. deficits—the very cause of the international monetary crises that led to the demise of Bretton Woods.

On Domestic Dreams and International Nightmares The notion that governments can divorce domestic inflation from international economics is fallacious. There is no domestic-international dichotomy in economic theory. There is a causal relationship between all economic activities, thus there can be no international immunity from unsound domestic policies and no domestic immunity from unsound international policies.

To the degree that nations practice sound domestic economic and monetary policies, the result will be stable economic progress in both the domestic and international economies. To the degree that domestic policies are unsound, distortions will occur that will be destabilizing and inhibit economic progress both domestically and internationally—the results being counterproductive in both areas. Bretton Woods was set up to accommodate various nations' domestic dreams. The dreams of postwar prosperity were financed by inflationary schemes that were incompatible with any sound international monetary standard. The Bretton Woods agreement established the contradictory system of fixed exchange rates with a built-in devaluation mechanism, in order to avert the monetary repercussions of not adhering to the exchange rates they fixed.

The framers of Bretton Woods knew that governments had no intention of preserving the value of their currencies, that, in fact, they planned to deficit spend and inflate in order to pay for their domestic economic programs.

No international monetary system—not the gold standard nor any form of a standardless fiat system, nor any combination thereof—can insure stability given unsound domestic policies. The fundamental economic issue today is not the kind of international monetary system that will replace the Bretton Woods system, but whether the domestic policies of the nations involved will permit any international monetary system to last. The precondition of any lasting monetary system is that it has integrity.

A monetary system that has integrity means a monetary system that is protected from government-created inflation; that is, arbitrary and artificial increases in the supply of money and credit.

It is a moral indictment against today's political leaders and the public at large that the chances for a monetary system that has integrity are almost nonexistent. Before a nation can have a monetary system of integrity, it must end all policies of inflationary finance. This means that all those dreams a nation cannot afford must end.

The public has bought the politician's claim that they can get something for nothing; that all a government need do is print up money to pay for programs that satisfy national dreams. But there is no such thing as a free lunch—someone must inevitably pay the price of that lunch.

And so it is with domestic dreams. The price for indulging in domestic dreams through government something-for-nothing programs is domestic inflation and international monetary crises with all their tragic and disruptive consequences.

If the domestic dreams of nations today are pursued by resorting to the insidious schemes of inflationary finance, they will inevitably become the international nightmares of tomorrow.

This was the lesson learned from the Bretton Woods system. May it rest in peace.

Chapter 8

Who's Protected by Protectionism?

Free trade is essential to the gold standard. Without it there would be no mechanism by which money could flow between nations. Further, protectionism is as dangerous a policy as there is. It has often led to trade wars. No one wins a trade war—everyone loses.

The case for free trade has never been refuted. Since the days of Adam Smith, most economists have understood and documented its virtues. Yet, the world has never known unrestricted free trade. Why?

One reason is the popular acceptance of the mythical virtues of mercantilism. Mercantilism is a government policy aimed at preventing individuals from purchasing goods abroad while encouraging them to sell goods abroad.

Mercantilism holds that a nation that exports (loses goods) is better off than one that imports (gains goods). It has been proven a hundred times over that it is detrimental for a nation to continuously export more than it imports. When government prevents or discourages individuals from purchasing goods abroad and encourages chronic exports, it limits a nation's supply of goods and encourages a decline in its citizens' standard of living.

Government control and regulation of international trade inevitably causes major economic distortions both domestically and internationally. The idea that we can all be, and should all be, sellers is preposterous. There must be consumers as well as sellers. Equilibrium is the state where both come together. The goal of mercantilism is to prevent this from occurring.

But mercantilism is never advocated for its own sake or as a viable economic policy. Rather, it enters the economy through the back door as a political policy of protectionism. Politicians are asked to protect the balance of trade, to protect the domestic market, or to protect domestic jobs and wages. But when implemented, the policy of protectionism is not a defensive move by government; it is an aggressive policy designed to penalize the best of producers by reducing or eliminating the high quality and/or low priced products they provide consumers.

Protectionism is a policy that excludes or reduces competition. Beneficiaries of such government aggression can only be the monopolists or quasi-monopolists that feed off government favors. Such businesses can exist only by government's power to force all competitors out of a given market, and this is always at the expense of consumers who are forced to accept artificially higher priced and/or lower quality goods. Some nations actually prevent their citizens from buying particular products or taking their money outside of their country.

Such protectionist policies have gained support only because most individuals believe they are necessary and that the policies do, in fact, protect them. But nothing is farther from the truth. To understand why protectionism does not protect individuals' economic interests and why it is totally unnecessary to the economic well-being of a nation, it is best to review a few basic principles of free trade. Unfortunately these time-tested truisms have been lost to the world for many years now.

A Few Principles

Suppose Smith and Jones are the only inhabitants of an island. Smith excels in farming and Jones excels in fishing. Smith may choose to devote his time to farming, while Jones may choose to devote his time to fishing. Assuming that Jones desires agricultural goods and Smith desires fish, a basis for trade exists when each produces more than sufficient goods for his own use. Thus, both gain by specializing in their own lines of production. This is called the principle of "specialization of production," and through such specialization the standard of living of both Smith and Jones increases.

But what happens if Smith and Jones both decide to catch fish? Even if Jones is superior to Smith in the art of catching fish, Jones has no reason to trade his surplus fish to Smith, since Smith has nothing to trade except other fish. Obviously if they trade fish for fish (all fish remaining equal), there can be no gain to either. Clearly, it would benefit Smith to return to farming where he could have his fruits and vegetables plus fish. This is called the principle of "division of labor."

But suppose Jones is superior to Smith in both farming and fishing. Will trade cease to exist? Not at all. It will pay Jones to specialize in the line of production in which he has the greatest "comparative advantage." In other words, if Jones can catch ten fish per day compared to Smith's five fish and produce ten baskets of berries compared to Smith's eight baskets, it will pay Jones to catch fish. Jones is free to devote himself exclusively to what he is relatively superior (competitive) at doing. In this way, part of his ten fish can be exchanged for part of Smith's eight baskets of berries. Smith and Jones, jointly, are therefore producing 10 fish and eight baskets of berries rather than five fish and 10 baskets of berries. Production is maximized, trade is increased, and the standard of living of both Smith and Jones is higher.

Enter Protectionism

Now, add two policemen to the island. Each will supply the service of protection—one protecting Smith, the other Jones. As a part of Smith's police protection, suppose that the Smith government imposes a restriction on Jones' fish, namely, a limit on the amount of fish that Smith can consume (import); or suppose a tariff is levied on Jones' fish, that is, the price (the amount of berries exchanged for fish) is increased to discourage Smith from consuming Jones' fish. Will such protection improve Smith's living conditions? The justification for this protection is that it will allegedly stimulate Smith's employment and production. Think about it.

While it is true that Smith will have to work longer in order to produce the fish once supplied by Jones, this will not raise Smith's standard of living. On the contrary, Smith's standard of living will be lowered. Smith must suffer either a reduction of fish or increase his labor to obtain the same amount of fish he would otherwise receive in trade from Jones.

The above example is extremely simplistic; yet, the principles, when applied to more complex economic conditions, hold true for all levels of trade—from the level of our gross-island-product example to international dealings. While the concrete specifics and the motives of protectors may vary, the result remains the same.

Specialization of production, the division of labor, and the principles of comparative advantage are undisputed economic laws that will always and everywhere increase a nation's standard of living. Conversely, trade restrictions, such as quotas and tariffs, only serve to reduce trade between individuals and, thus, to reduce their standard of living.

It is claimed that if we protect our manufacturing industry, jobs will be created here at home and employment will rise. This is true. But only a small percent of us work in the manufacturing industry. While it is possible to help an individual or an industry, it must come at the expense of another individual or industry. At the end of the day protection hurts a nation at large, even though it may protect a small group of individuals for a while.

Trade between Nations

No nation on earth possesses all the conditions necessary for producing all goods. Geographical conditions, climate, and resources vary widely. For instance, some countries are more suited to produce coffee, others steel, others oil, wheat, or microchips. As each nation specializes in the products that, given its particular conditions, are to its comparative advantage to produce, world trade will increase and all trading partners will benefit.

Consider the reverse effect. What would happen to trade and the standard of living for the citizens of the United States if citizens between states were prevented from trading with each other? Oregon produces lumber; Pennsylvania produces steel; Florida produces oranges. What if each state imposed tariffs and quotas on all imports or prevented its people from importing? Would the standard of living of the citizens in these states rise? Obviously not; it would fall as the volume of trade fell and as individuals were forced to reduce consumption or spend more time to produce that which they desired or needed to live—assuming they could.

Consumption would drop as many products were eliminated from markets or rose in price, shutting out less wealthy consumers. The same principle would hold true for international trade; protectionism reduces world production and consumption.

The case for international trade and against protectionism is that simple and that powerful. Yet, the world has never experienced completely free trade. Why? Here are a few of the most popular arguments for protectionism.

To Protect the Balance of Trade Nations have continuously endeavored to achieve a favorable balance of trade despite the fact that all the evidence suggests a favorable balance of trade is unfavorable. Trade is supposed to be favorable when a nation is continuously exporting more goods than it imports. This results in more money entering the domestic economy from foreign markets and less money leaving the domestic economy as the nation buys fewer goods abroad.

Without government encouragement (coercion), an increase of exports over imports will not last long. When a nation sells more goods abroad, domestic prices rise as its money supply increases.

When this occurs, foreigners curtail their purchases; the higher domestic prices entice citizens of the exporting nation to look elsewhere and to begin importing. As imports increase and exports decrease, money begins to leave the economy and prices begin to fall. This restores equilibrium to the domestic price structure and to the balance of trade.

This was the case under the classic gold standard. As long as nations adhered to the rules of the gold standard and allowed the free flow of capital and goods, equilibrium was always restored.

But the mercantilist government will settle for nothing less than a favorable balance of trade—which is not a balance at all, but an imbalanced trade surplus. Government steps into the economy to protect its citizens from foreign goods. It institutionalizes such restrictions as tariffs and quotas that protect individuals from the bargain prices abroad. Government artificially reduces (devalues) the worth of its monetary unit and, through controls and regulations, creates an artificial situation that entices individuals to continue selling goods abroad. As the goods (the wealth) of a nation are drained, its citizens are prevented from using the money they receive for these goods to purchase lower priced and/or better quality goods abroad. It is then that government proudly announces the achievement of a favorable balance of trade.

Who is protected by this protectionism? No one; there are a few who may benefit (such as those in the artificially stimulated export industry) but it will be at the expense of the consumer. Remember, we are all consumers. All individuals will suffer— either through generally higher prices or lower quality goods. Thus the government has succeeded in forcibly reducing everyone's economic choices, as well as their standard of living.

To Protect Domestic Markets One of the most popular arguments for protectionism is that, without tariffs, certain domestic industries would lose their markets to foreign competitors. This is true, but what does it mean? It means that some firm or industry abroad can satisfy consumer needs and desires better than the home industry. It means that some company can produce a better product or produce the same product at a lower cost. When an industry asks for protection, it is not asking for the defensive powers of government—it is asking for the aggressive powers of government to force taxpayers to subsidize its inability to compete. It is asking the government to subsidize inefficiency. This must always be at the expense of the consumer, for it means imposing tariffs (taxes) on foreign products that enable the home industry to charge relatively lower prices and appear competitive; but competitive only because the prices on foreign products have been artificially increased by tariffs.

"But if we don't protect our home industry, imports will flood our markets and we'll surely have mass unemployment." This would be an alarming fact if it was true, but it is not. What is not seen is that the import industry will increase *their* employment. Why is employment in the import industry bad and employment in the export industry good? Who is protected by protecting domestic markets? Usually it is the export industry, at the expense of the import industry. Do you ever wonder why the export industry is always in the news and the import industry is rarely mentioned? Perhaps it depends on the size of the gang you have to gain political favors.

To Protect Domestic Wages It is often argued that lower wage countries are a competitive threat to higher wage nations. It is argued that if higher wages are not protected by tariffs and quotas on foreign goods, wages will surely fall, lowering the standard of living of millions of workers.

But why are wages higher in some countries than in others? The reason is productivity. For example, U.S. workers are paid the highest wages in the world. This is because the U.S. worker produces more per day than the average worker in other nations. Suppose a foreign worker's wage is a dollar per hour while a U.S. worker's wage is ten dollars per hour. It would seem that this high wage rate would increase the final price of the product. But this is not so if the American worker is producing ten times more than his foreign competitor. And the fact is, the American worker is far more productive than workers in other nations.

Protectionists would have you believe that cheap labor is a threat to high wage nations. The fact is that cheap labor is cheap because it produces so much less. Given U.S. efficiency, capital, machinery, technology, and mass production techniques, the cost per unit of output is lower in the United States than in other countries.

Thus, higher U.S. wages merely reflect greater U.S. productivity; they do not necessarily result in higher prices. And lower wages usually reflect less productivity, but will not necessarily result in lower prices. Anyone living in California can tell you it costs less to eat at a fast food restaurant in the United States than in Mexico.

Once again, protectionism penalizes the efficient and competent foreign producers (and therefore the American consumer) while rewarding incompetent or inefficient domestic producers. Protectionism does not protect domestic wages; it simply allows incompetence to grow and thrive where it could never exist without government protection. And once again, consumers pay for such protectionism by being forced to pay higher prices and accept lower-quality goods.

Protectionism: The Greatest Threat to Prosperity Trade wars pose the most devastating economic threat there is to the economies of the world. They come disguised as protection for workers and consumers. Grab your wallet and run every time you hear they may be imposed. Here are a few of the more common forms of protectionism:

- Licensing restrictions force individuals to apply for permission to export or import. They are an effective way to curtail trade. They are a blatant use of government force intended to control free people who peacefully want to trade with one another. They are often associated with what is called an industrial policy. This is where the government tells us all what is best for us. They take over trade as a tool of foreign and economic policy rather than allowing the free market to operate. This policy is usually accompanied by slogans claiming that the free market has failed or the policy is cloaked in nationalism, appealing to the patriotism of producers and consumers.

- Import quotas prevent individuals from purchasing goods from abroad. The government decrees that no goods (or only so much of a particular good) may be purchased from one or more nations. What do import quotas cost? They cost economic variety. Individual economic choices are reduced since import quotas amount to blockades against consumer demands. This contracts world trade, which further reduces people's standard of living.

- Tariffs are artificially higher prices paid for international goods. Government imposes tariffs to discourage imports and sometimes to increase revenues. Tariffs are taxes. When individuals purchase foreign goods at their neighborhood stores, they pay additional money for these goods equaling the government-imposed tax. This costs economic variety, as foreign goods are unable to mount the government's tariff wall. This leads to a contraction of world trade and to higher prices.
- Import surcharges are usually across-the-board tariffs on all imports. In 1971 a temporary 20 percent import surcharge was imposed on American citizens. This 20 percent tax was hailed by government as a diplomatic coup and cheered patriotically by citizens. Protective tariffs seem to be the only taxes people cheer. The amazing sight of individuals cheering their own taxation indicates how blindly they have accepted the myths of protectionism.

There is one other protectionist measure that should be mentioned. Our protectors believe it represents a threat to individuals. The word used to designate this threat brings fear into the hearts of government officials at its mere mention: the word is dumping.

Since just about every government in the world accepts the favorable balance of trade theory as gospel, politicians fear that some other nation may try to flood their nation with cheap goods. Dumping occurs when an industry sells its product below the market price to a foreign nation. This, of course, results in individuals purchasing these goods at bargain prices (poor devils!) and hurts that nation's trade position. It is as if charging less than market prices is an act of aggression. To guard against it we have established treaties between nations to prevent such crises.

The U.S. Balance of Payments Problem in Perspective

Today, we all know that the United States has been running large trade deficits for years. Most believe that trade deficits are inherently bad. The fact is that if there is a gain to a nation who's running trade imbalances, it is on the deficit side. Consider it. We give the world our dollars; they give us their goods. More goods at cheaper prices increase our living standard.

Normally, under the rules of a gold standard and free trade, the money foreigners receive would be used to purchase American goods. That is what the money is for! But because their governments prevent the producers of wealth from trading for other wealth, they are forced to live on only what they and their countrymen produce.

Like Smith and Jones on the island, they are confined by their limited ability to trade. And at the end of the day they are poorer for it. The best way to resolve our trade problems and the distortions that accompany them is to go directly to the people of protectionist nations and explain to them why they are not being protected by protectionism. Perhaps then they will kick their protectors out of office in favor of a more free trade policy and the world can return to equilibrium.

The Protection Racket One fact should be crystal clear at this point; it is not protection that protectionism offers—it is aggression. The government violates individual rights for the sake of providing illegitimate gains for certain special interest groups. While government offers the above myths as proof of why individuals would be defenseless without policies of protectionism, it goes coercively on its way violating the very rights it is supposed to preserve. In no way does protectionism protect the lives, property, or the liberty of individuals. It is a government policy that can exist only by government-initiated force against most individuals. Protectionism has always existed to some degree, and so long as individuals hold the above myths as indisputable facts, the protection racket is safe.

The protection racket breeds on ignorance and thrives on the tactics of pressure group warfare. It is a disease that spreads with every collectivist slogan advocating the right of some individuals to be defended at the expense of other individuals. It is clothed in fashionable phrases and trimmed with patriotic jargon, but underneath this superficial disguise is the decayed body of a doctrine that can exist only by virtue of government force.

It is the enemy of the gold standard, capitalism, freedom, and world prosperity. As such, protectionism is the enemy of all individuals.

Part III

RETURNING TO A GOLD STANDARD

Chapter 9

Are the Fiat and the Gold Standards Converging?

L et's start from a premise that we have pure capitalism, which means there is no government involvement in the economy. Government laws, controls, and regulations are totally designed to protect individual rights and property rights; to prevent force and fraud through the establishment of armies and police; to establish a court system where disputes can be resolved and crimes prosecuted; and to establish standards and rules of the road in order to conduct transactions consistent with these goals. This means we would be living in a nation of totally free markets. Assuming individuals chose gold as their medium of exchange, as they have most of the time over the last 2,500 years, the supply and value of money would be determined by the market, not government as it is today under a fiat standard.

Under a gold standard, the money supply is determined by the amount of gold produced. Credit is determined by the amount of deposits banks receive for savings. Banks lend out what is deposited, on a short-term to long-term basis. Since there is a risk that depositors may want to withdraw their savings at any time, they must keep sufficient reserves on hand to cover any withdrawals on demand. The market, over decades of the gold standard, determined that a prudent reserve ratio was about three or four to one. Thus, leverage was always contained and so was credit expansion. The amount of paper claims to gold was always limited.

A fiat standard, as envisioned by the late Milton Friedman, would have the government rather than the market determine the quantity of money and credit. Friedman would set the money supply at 3 to 5 percent, where he believed price stability would be ensured. Notice that under both systems the goals are price stability, limited credit expansion, and optimum economic growth.

The fact is, we have had financial panics under both the gold standard, such as in 1907, and the government-controlled fiat standard of today. But under the gold standard, the value of the dollar remained stable nationally and internationally for a hundred years with few exceptions. Since 1913, when the Fed took over the control of the money supply, the dollar has fallen to about three cents of its previous value and is depreciating further as we speak. If preserving the value of money is the standard by which to judge a monetary system, the fiat standard has been a dismal failure, where the gold standard has succeeded.

A Monetary System Needs to Know Its Limitations

During the reign of the gold standard, money supply did what Professor Friedman wanted the fiat standard to do: It increased at a low and stable rate. Under the fiat standard the money supply has exploded at times as it has today. The big difference is that gold increases were dependent on finding and mining gold where under a fiat standard the quantity of money is arbitrarily determined by government officials. Friedman's solution to this problem is simple: Replace the Fed Open Market Committee with a computer. Make the money supply increase automatically and consistently. By suggesting this, Friedman was conceding that the best a fiat standard could do was to mimic a gold standard.

Leverage existed under the gold standard but was restrained by the fact that at the first sign of any banking problem, depositors would begin to lose confidence. This would result in an immediate run on the bank in question as depositors turned in their paper claims to gold and withdrew the gold itself. The fact of convertibility kept leverage low.

However, even with low leverage, speculation and panics can occur. In 1907 we had a financial run on banks that almost brought the entire financial system of America tumbling down. J.P. Morgan rallied a handful of millionaires and eventually saved the system by restoring confidence on Wall Street as well as on Main Street. It was then that a call for a stronger bank of last resort was urged and six years later the Fed was created.

The idea of a strong national bank is not new. It was vigorously debated by Alexander Hamilton and Thomas Jefferson. Hamilton ended up winning that argument. The idea is not a bad one. In its purest form it argues that a bank with huge reserves on hand should at all times stand ready to back up any institution that threatens to bring down the financial system. In 1907 it was a handful of extremely rich investors that served this function. In the 1980s it was the Federal Deposit Insurance Corporation (FDIC), which collects fees from banks to back up the strong banks by helping them absorb the bad banks. And in 2007 and 2008 it was the Treasury and Fed that played that role with the backing of the U.S. taxpayer.

Where the money of the bank of last resort comes from becomes a crucial point. U.S. bonds are backed by the "full faith and credit of the U.S. government." That's us, folks! We, the taxpayer, are the backers of bonds. Should we also be the backers of a bank of last resort? My own view is that the idea of a bank of last resort is a good one but it should be funded by those most likely to cause structural damage to the economic and monetary system. The dues paid into the FDIC by all banks have worked well as an insurance policy and backstop for banks that go bad. Many banks within that system have failed but without structural damage to the system as a whole, and depositors have remained relatively unburdened by their internal problems.

The regulations and government agencies that were put in place after 1907 and into the 1930s were all designed to prevent what has happened today. Some worked well, such as the FDIC insurance program. Some were and are totally worthless. The attempt to update the regulatory architecture of the financial system is being written, and to some extent, implemented now. Many of the proposals will become law over the years. I am for regulatory reform. I think we need reform given the massive fraud that was allowed to occur during the last several years. But as sure as I am that we need regulatory reform, I also am absolutely sure that regulatory reform will not prevent a future panic and crisis, such as the one we've just had, from happening in the future.

But just because you can't rid society of criminals doesn't mean we should have bad or useless laws on the books. And the regulatory laws and agencies we have today definitely need inspection. One area that needs a hard look is the use of leverage.

Reduced Leverage Equals Reduced Speculation

Most people agree that some kind of rules need to be established when it comes to leverage. For example, we have had margin requirements on stocks since the crash of 1929 and they have worked pretty well. Under the gold standard the 4:1 leverage rule of banks did not prevent runs, but the downside risk was much less than it would have been at 100:1 leverage. You can't get hurt much falling out of a one-story apartment, but you can get killed falling out of a skyscraper. A move back toward gold standard leverage ratios would be a move in the right direction. And it appears to me this is the direction we are moving in. Higher capital requirements—the other side of the leverage coin—are being discussed in all nations around the world.

Another reform being proposed is the creation of a separate regulatory body to relieve the Fed of that responsibility. I think that makes sense. It is the government's job to police fraud and prosecute the violation of rules and regulations, not the Fed's. The Fed should simply set monetary policy and operate as a bank of last resort. It should, in my opinion, set the money supply at a low and stable level and allow the Federal Funds rate and all interest rates to seek their own level. As bank of last resort it should naturally monitor any abuses of the system that threaten systemic damage and assist the government in monitoring risk. But the Fed cannot, nor should it try to, be a policeman.

The Process of Convergence

It is interesting that over the years the fiat standard and the gold standard have been slowly converging. A move in the above proposed direction would move both systems even closer. Just as Milton Friedman's vision of a fiat standard shared many of the same goals of the gold standard, the two systems can, have been, and are, converging to some degree. Consider the following:

Over the years the fiat standard has become more gold-oriented. The first major move was the re-legalization of gold in 1975. For the first time since 1933, individuals were allowed to own gold. Gold ownership is a necessary condition of a gold standard. It offers individuals a choice of wealth preservation. They can choose to save in paper dollars or ounces of gold. It was the first step in the defense against the debasement of the currency. This moved us closer to a gold standard within the context of a fiat standard.

In the 1970s, inflation was hidden. Few understood the relationship of an increase in money supply and rising prices. But Milton Friedman established and sold that relationship to the economic community as well as the public at large. His clear and simple explanations took the dismal science and made it intelligible to the average citizen. The result of this new understanding of the cause of inflation led to a further accumulation of gold by individuals and governments alike.

Today, inflation is no longer an esoteric phenomenon. It is understood by most Americans. As a result, the Fed's option to inflate has decreased. During the 1970s we experienced progressive inflation as the Fed progressively increased the money supply for a decade. The result was an inflation rate that progressively climbed from 2 percent to 12 percent by 1980. Paul Volcker ended that era. One of the pillars of Reaganomics was a strong dollar and a sound monetary policy. From that time to now, the inflation rate has progressively declined from 12 percent to an average of about 3 percent, to almost zero today. We have even at times experienced a little deflation.

Today's calls for the reduction in the Fed's independence, greater transparency, and even the elimination of the Fed itself by some, would never have happened in the 1970s. The alarm among economists of a soaring Fed balance sheet of over two trillion dollars and the calls by Wall Street to delineate a Fed exit strategy stands as a check on Fed actions. Further, the existence of hundreds of TV and radio commentators, together with newsletter writers and bloggers warning of possible future inflation, reduces the power of the Fed. If it were not for the economic and monetary emergency we faced, I seriously doubt any such huge increase in money supply would ever be tolerated. Today there are a million prying eyes on the Fed and the money supply, where in the 1970s there were not.

In addition, there is a keen awareness of the importance that credit expansion and leverage played in creating the panic of 2007 and 2008. Congress and the U.S. Treasury, as well as the Fed, are now considering controls on credit expansion. This ideological move toward reducing the money supply as well as reducing credit, debt creation, and leverage, is a move toward the kind of monetary system a gold standard would provide.

I am not suggesting that we are returning to the gold standard. But I am suggesting we are moving toward it.

Gold has been mobilized. It is moving into the hands of investors and savers all over the world. It is being rediscovered by central banks as a currency of last resort. Gold reserves are being increased rather than decreased as they were just a few years ago by most government central banks. And paper currency is being sold for gold all over the world. Gold as a reserve asset among governments, and a preferred asset among individuals, investors, and institutions, is once again in vogue.

And every day that the value of the dollar drops on international markets, there are fresh calls for the need for a stable reserve currency. The dollar continues to become less desirable and gold more desirable to satisfy that function. This, I submit, is a reduction in the confidence of the fiat standard and an increase in the interest gold can play in the monetary systems throughout the world. As we speak, individuals in every corner of the world are trading paper for gold. And this trend, in my opinion, is not a fad. I give you the huge increase in gold Exchange Traded Funds in the last five years as just one example.

A New Day

Next, consider the level of education among newsletter writers and media commentators. It is greater today than at any time in my lifetime. There is very little that is not understood today about money and economics. There are strong disagreements to be sure. And there is an intellectual battle taking place daily. But the ideas are out there. They are being debated.

The degree to which we move toward a gold standard will depend a lot on how this debate plays out and how the Fed performs over the next few years. It will be one thing if it pulls off a fairly smooth transition from a near-meltdown to a return to monetary stability without creating any major inflation. It will be quite another thing if it does not.

The Fed definitely has its work cut out for it. If the Fed pulls off a smooth transition from its emergency lending strategy of two trillion dollars of new money without causing inflation or any major disruptions, the fiat standard will emerge as a stronger, more credible system than ever before. But it may only be able to do so by moving toward the principles of a gold standard. If we increase capital requirements and reduce leverage, increase gold within the central banks as reserves and within public hands as savings, commit to low and stable rates of money growth, and establish interest rates that are market originated, we will end up with a stronger and more predictable monetary system than we've had since the nineteenth century.

The movement today to deal with systemic risk is an attempt to approximate the conditions of a free market and a gold standard without allowing them to completely exist. For each market action that is not allowed to happen government must invent a rule or regulation to compensate for it. For example, in the absence of the conservative reserve ratio's adopted by banks in the nineteenth century we are talking about government imposing greater capital requirements on banks in the twenty-first century. In a perverse way we are being forced by reality to move closer to free market and gold standard principles of conduct without calling it that.

To summarize, the megatrend is the following:

1. Gold is returning to portfolios and government coffers as speculative risk assets are being reduced. Central banks are buying gold for the first time in decades instead of selling. We are moving slowly toward a de facto gold standard.

2. The Fed's and the public's understanding of what causes inflation have served to reduce the increase of money supply over the last three decades. We no longer have hidden inflation. We have open inflation and, as such, the insidious nature of theft by inflation is much more obvious and much less probable. Everyone is on the lookout for inflation, as evidenced by the countless commercials for gold.

3. The mindset of Congress is to redouble their efforts to enforce laws against fraud, deceit, and excess leverage, a necessity for a sound monetary system.

4. The intellectual movement worldwide toward free market capitalism is flourishing, as witnessed by the free market tendencies of China, Russia, and Eastern Europe.

5. The money supply as defined by M1, the only "M" that the Fed directly controls, grew at 7 to 8 percent rates in the late 1970s. M1 was brought down substantially since then and was held at zero in 2005, 2006, 2007, and most of 2008. This indicates the degree to which monetary philosophy has changed over the years. It is true that the Fed recently exploded their balance sheet, but that was an emergency move in an attempt to replace the money lost through deleveraging in financial institutions. It has been the exception in monetary policy, not the rule. And it could not be accomplished without it being open to the public and the promise of an exit policy to assure the public and the markets that inflation was not the goal. It was initiated as a temporary emergency measure, not a change in policy.

6. The price index defined by the CPI fell from 12 percent to very low levels over the last 30 years. You may want to question the efficacy of the CPI, but you cannot question the direction. In fact, from time to time, we actually had a little deflation.

If, indeed, we move toward greater stability of the money supply, open and market originated interest rates, and greater enforcement of laws against fraud, deceit, and leverage, we will have improved our monetary system and created a more stable system of honest money. Not a bad move. And a move in the right direction, I might add.

Chapter 10

Gold: The New Money

The use of the terms gold standard and new reserve currency are being used more in the last year than in the last few decades. Perhaps that is the tip-off. Some commentators, writers, and magazines are beginning to join the debate on the pros and cons of a return to the gold standard. One said he would bet his career that this will never happen. Most laugh at the prospect. The fact is it is happening now.

The new controversy over reverting to a gold standard is welcome. Many who comment, pro and con, on the possibility are new to the subject, and as such have not really thought through some of the implications. I have been writing articles on the gold standard since the early 1970s, and I welcome the new commentators to this debate.

Two points I would like to make to anyone who participates: One: Any return to a gold standard will come well into the future. A return to the gold standard will be incremental. You cannot graft a gold standard onto the present system. It presupposes fiscal responsibility, balanced budgets, monetary stability, and free trade. A political and economic transformation would need to occur first. Two: It will look much different from gold standards of the past. No one knows—or can know—what a future gold standard will look like. The reason is that technology has changed.

Today we can compute values of gold, silver, copper, or anything else and convert those values into paper claims in a nanosecond. Which means we could pay for goods and services with a credit or debit card, which is backed by our savings or checking accounts. Which means we could save in gold or silver and use the credit or debit card as our medium of exchange.

My suggestion to all those wanting to return to gold is that the best way to accomplish this is not by proclaiming your determination to replace the Federal Reserve Board with the gold standard but to attack the legal tender laws of this country. I was one of the few back in the early 1970s that fought for the legalization of gold to be allowed back into the American system. That was the first step in returning to the gold standard. Today is very much the same. The next step is to institutionalize competing monies. Today's technology will allow us to do this effectively.

The key is to go after the government's monopoly on money. If broken, gold will find its way into the monetary system, as it is today, and reclaim its superior role as long as it is not prevented from doing so. Legal tender laws do just that.

Today, to be an advocate of a gold standard is to be laughed at and ridiculed as naive. But to be against legal tender laws wipes the snickers off the faces of those against gold very quickly. To be against legal tender laws is to be for freedom and against government coercion. You will not find the same chuckles from intellectuals when confronted with a proposal of this nature. On the contrary, you will find terror.

This goes to the heart of government power. It goes to the use of force. It goes to government's ability to control people, raise taxes, borrow money, and inflate. This is the tactic and strategy required to achieve an honest money once again in this country. Let the private market develop a private money and compete with government money, and then we will see who has money and who does not.

Rediscovering Gold

Government has a monopoly on money. It declares what can and cannot be legal tender. It controls the value of money through setting the supply and the price of money by setting short-term interest rates. We have been on a fiat standard for a century. Fiat means decree and that is what government does—sometimes subtly, sometimes brutally. But make no mistake, the government controls money.

The force of a monopoly alone, however, is insufficient to prevent individuals from protecting their wealth. So, government's best chance of preserving stability is through trust, confidence, and credibility. Lose these things and government will eventually lose control. Today, we see this very scenario playing out before our eyes.

Over the last few years, there has been a move away from government money and towards gold. Not too long ago, governments were net sellers of gold. Every year they would announce how much gold they were going to sell into the market. It was part of demonetization, which represented a monetary philosophy that accepted the fact that gold was a barbarous relic that had little relevance in today's modern financial system. If governments needed money, they would simply print it. If they needed more gold, they would print that too. They created paper gold, known as Special Drawing Rights, or SDRs. These would act as reserves instead of the metal itself.

The International "Walk" on Gold

Flash forward. Today, there is a steady run on gold by a growing number of governments everywhere. It is not a panic run it is more subtle and incremental than that. As creditor nations begin to question the value of their paper reserves they have begun converting them into gold. Gold is becoming, once again, the reserve currency of the world banking system.

More importantly, individuals are beginning to accumulate gold. In five years the ETF that tracks the price of gold, the SPDR Gold Trust (GLD), has bought more and more gold as demand has risen. It now holds more gold in trust for individuals than most governments do. And gold coin sales are breaking records throughout the world as individuals clamor to own physical gold. This is the re-monetization of gold. Yet only a fraction of individuals still actually own gold.

The free market is a marvelous thing to behold. It has a life of its own. It represents the values and judgments of free individuals—right or wrong—apart from government decree or informed opinion. Even in dictatorships you will find black markets where you can find pretty much anything you want for a price. So when you see a trend—as you do today—toward gold accumulation, you need to take notice. What is it telling us?

Personally, I view it as a market response to the need for an honest currency outside the influence of governments. At a time when government debt, currencies, and financial institutions are all under suspicion, is it any wonder that the market demands an historic form of money, devoid of government influence and promises? That demand is being sought out and satisfied daily.

Many investors look at the price of gold and claim it is in a bubble. But it is not a matter of price—it is a matter of possession. If only a fraction of individuals around the world posses gold today, what would a future price of gold be when almost everyone wanted gold?

If governments fail to get their fiscal houses in order there is no telling what the future will bring. Gold offers some semblance of security. Among other things, it is a hedge against stupidity. Given the almost criminally reckless fiscal policies of government, who in their right mind would not want to protect themselves? And if a breakdown of national currencies occurs, who would believe the promises of a new replacement paper currency in light of the broken promises of governments everywhere. Gold is not a promise that can be broken, and therein lies its present appeal.

Competing Monies

In my opinion the private market is in the process of developing a private competing money. No one can predict where this will lead us, but it is happening as we speak. We are seeing the emergence of gold ATMs whereby individuals can convert dollars for gold on demand. If those machines eventually are equipped to also accept gold for paper money, we will have the specter of convertibility on street corners everywhere.

Companies that buy gold are everywhere, and companies that sell gold are increasing. Convertibility is becoming an industry. This is a further sign of the establishment of the new private money.

How this will evolve, not even the market knows. But it is obvious the market is telling us that there is a demand for gold as money. Will we start computing commodity prices, stock values, and possibly all prices in terms of gold, as well as the dollar, to know whether we have deflation or inflation and to what degree? Will credit card companies start pricing and translating purchases of goods and services in terms of dollars and gold as they do foreign currencies? Will financial institutions store gold as a new form of savings account en masse? In a new world of modern technology there is no telling how gold will be used, but it is being explored by entrepreneurs worldwide as we speak.

To be sure, it will be a long time before we are walking around with gold, silver, nickel, and copper coins in our pockets as we did in the past; there is a long way to go before we ever see gold in the form of a medium of exchange. But there is little doubt that gold will be needed more by governments in the future to shore up their failing fiat standard and desired more by individuals as a money of last resort in case they don't.

In either case gold is back—and back big time. Those that argue that the price of gold is approximating a bubble miss the point. What if governments around the world lose the confidence of those that hold their paper money? What if individuals through the private market desire a nongovernmental money, as they are starting to today? What if the billions of individuals who do not own gold start to demand it? What price of gold then? Talk of a bubble within this context becomes meaningless and is way premature.

This is not a prediction of sky-high gold prices yet to come, but rather the realization that what we are experiencing is not a bubble in gold, but a steady increase in real demand.

To all the pundits that believe a gold standard is impractical, I suggest they look at the present fiat system that presided over the Roaring Twenties; the Great Depression of the thirties; the hundreds of devaluations under the Bretton Woods system of the forties, fifties, and sixties; the stagflation of the 1970s; and the demise of WorldCom, Enron, and Lehman Brothers culminating in one of the greatest financial crises of all times, and then judge it against the hundred years of monetary stability we enjoyed in years past under the gold standard. Then talk to me about which system is practical and which system is not.

Chapter 11

How *Not* to Advocate
a Gold Standard*

T oday, there is a growing interest in gold in general and the gold standard in particular as a replacement for the fiat standard that has failed so miserably over the past century. Yet any attempt at returning to the gold standard is being undermined by statements containing a host of errors, inconsistencies, and contradictions about gold—statements made by those very individuals who are attempting to focus attention on gold and the virtues of a gold standard.

---

*This article was reprinted from *The Freeman*, published by The Foundation for Economic Education in August 1973.

A bad argument advocating a return to the gold standard can be more harmful to the case for gold than no argument at all.

One source of such arguments is that many gold advocates look at gold through the eyes of an investor rather than the eyes of an economist. Consequently, short-term, superficial, and sometimes misleading interest in gold is being encouraged at the expense of long-term education and consistent economic theory. This approach must ultimately be counterproductive and self-defeating. The market is being saturated with literature containing misconceptions and inexact or incorrect terminology. This has led to anti-gold positions (i.e., positions inconsistent with capitalism and a free market), most of which can be traced to poorly defined concepts, discussions drawn out of context, and misidentified cause/effect relationships. The following arguments, terms, and positions regarding gold, its present role in international monetary matters, and its proposed role in future international monetary reform, have presented a recurring yet self-defeating defense of gold and the gold standard.

The Intrinsic Worth Argument

It has been said that gold has intrinsic worth. This argument represents a theory of economics inconsistent with the free market and consequently with the gold standard.

The intrinsic theory of value holds that worth or value is contained within an object. It holds that economic goods possess value inherently, innately, despite the market, despite supply and demand, that is, in spite of individual's values, choices, and actions.

Free market economists reject this argument. They hold that no person can jump outside the market and declare what a particular commodity is worth; that all commodities are subject to the

130

laws of supply and demand; that in economics there is no such thing as intrinsic worth, only market worth.

Worth means value and value presupposes a valuer. As people's values differ and change, market values change. As supply and demand conditions change, the exchange ratios of commodities relative to one another change.

Gold is not exempt from these economic laws, and yet gold is often treated as if it were. By using such unscientific terms as intrinsic worth, the gold advocate can only hurt his own case—and he has. The inability of many gold advocates to objectively answer the question "Why gold?" has led to the misunderstanding of gold and to such popular terms as "gold, the mystic metal."

Gold would not be called mystic if it were understood. And understanding begins with defining one's terms. It is only through invalid concepts, such as intrinsic worth, that absurd terms such as mystic metal can gain popularity.

The Store of Value Argument

The argument that gold is a store of value is often used as a substitute for the intrinsic worth argument. Unless precisely qualified, the term can lead to the same errors, fallacies, and fallacious theories of the intrinsic worth argument. Thus, it may lead to a misunderstanding of the nature of money and of a proper theory of value.

Store of value is a term often used by those who argue that gold will always represent a constant value, namely that gold is a fixed yardstick representing constant purchasing power. Implicit in this argument, once again, is the idea that gold is intrinsically valuable— immune from the laws of the market. Not so. The possibilities of gold strikes, gold shortages, fiat money inflation, depression and deflation, fluctuation of industrial demand, the relative market value of other commodities, and the differing knowledge, values, and expectations of individuals—all these factors have the potential of increasing or decreasing the value of gold for others.

Does this mean that under a gold standard the price index and the value of money will fluctuate? It certainly does. But this is precisely the beauty of the free market and the case for freedom— that prices are allowed to fluctuate freely, thereby corresponding to the constantly changing and diverse values of free people. The advocates of a free market are not Utopians—they are realists who recognize that there are no guarantees of economic security in this world; they are willing to accept the consequences of their action—and to accept the verdict of a free market.

The advocates of a free market are not willing to trade their freedom for security. The store of value argument offers people just such a trade. While a gold standard does offer individuals more stability of value than any other free monetary system, it does not offer individuals a constant value. There is no harm in stating that gold is a store of value so long as one knows and states exactly what is meant by the term—that gold has stability of value and represents perhaps the best monetary method of saving. Gold is historically an excellent store of wealth, but not a store of value. In a free society, one is certainly free to store that which one values, so long as it is understood that the value of one's savings is not immune from the influence of the market. Thus, within the context of a free market, the only legitimate meaning of store of value is a commodity that is extremely marketable and therefore best facilitates the exchange of goods and services.

Gold Price Predictions

One way pro-gold advocates have been trying to attract attention to gold is by arousing investor interest through predictions of a higher gold price. General estimates of prices are not by themselves harmful. For example, it was a reasonable assumption that, after having been artificially held down for 40 years, the price of gold would increase. But specific price predictions are indirectly harmful to the case for gold.

The case for gold is subsumed under the broader case for the free market. The advocates of free market economics and those economists concerned with economic theory take pride in the rigorous logic and objectivity of the case for the free market. But this pride is being undercut by illogical and visionary price predictions. The price of gold is determined by the values of those participating in the gold market. No person on earth, no group of mathematicians (no matter how many charts and graphs they employ), no computer on earth, is capable of knowing the values of all consumers and suppliers within the market. Therefore, to try to precisely predict something as specific as a price is impossible. The fact is, people's values are constantly changing, just as the factors of supply, demand, and costs are changing. People cannot have precise, prior knowledge of prices, and by pretending to they can only confuse and undercut the entire concept and basis of free market economic theory.

There is no place for crystal balls in science—and that includes the science of economics. Those attempting to attract attention to gold by making precise price predictions are contradicting and obscuring the meaning of the free market and therefore under-cutting the case for a gold standard.

The Legal Tender Argument

Many advocates of gold argue that if gold were made legal tender, not only would individuals be allowed to use gold as money, but this would necessarily lead to a gold standard. What is forgotten is that this country's legal tender laws are precisely what prevented citizens from using gold as money for years. Legal tender laws established the legal precedent of a coercive government mono-poly over the issuance and use of Federal Reserve Notes.

The free market economist does not contend that gold must be money. He contends only that money must be market originated. The case for the gold standard is part of the broader case for com-modity money. Consistent advocates of the gold standard hold that gold possesses those qualities and characteristics most conducive to the function of a medium of exchange, but they do not say that gold will forever be suitable as money. Neither do they hold that gold must be accepted as money whether people want to accept it or not. They do not ask for the police powers of state to enforce their idea of what money should be. Thus, they oppose legal tender laws.

Further, legal tender laws are not necessary. All that is neces-sary is that people possess the right of contract. For example, if a person contracts to pay 100 ounces of gold to another person who agrees to accept this sum in payment, the courts need only recognize what has been chosen as money and assure that the obligation be discharged.

Legal tender laws are not what are needed to return to a gold standard. On the contrary, they are one of the major factors that have prevented the world from returning to gold.

The Official Price of Gold Fetish

Many advocates of gold argue that an official price of gold is both necessary and desirable. This position accepts the premise of opponents of the gold standard: that legal tender laws should be established allowing governments to legally fix and regulate the value of money. The free market position rejects this premise. It holds that the medium of exchange should be market originated and market regulated—not government originated and government regulated. This means that the value of money should be determined on the free market—not dictated by government decree.

At this point, the official price advocate usually says, "But if the price of gold isn't fixed, then no one will know what money is worth." And in the sense of having precise, prior knowledge of gold's exchange value, this is true—just as it is true for all other commodity exchange values.

It is interesting to note that those who argue both that gold should be fixed in value and that gold is a constant store of value hold a contradictory position in which one claim offsets the other. If gold is already a constant store of value, why should its price be fixed? And if it is necessary and desirable to fix the price of gold, then how can it be argued that gold has an intrinsically constant value? One need not fix that which is constant, and that which one does fix cannot be defined as constant. Such inconsistency pervades pro-gold literature today. In fact, what is being advocated is that gold should be a fixed yardstick—a constant store of value—by government directive, rather than a stable store of value by market directive. Government determination to fix the purchasing power of the monetary unit ignores, contradicts, and denies the law of the market.

Under a gold standard, no official price of gold would exist, hence no official store of value. But this does not mean that gold offers no stability of value. On the contrary, gold has been chosen by individuals as a medium of exchange for over 2,500 years precisely because of its stability of value. But market determined stability must be distinguished from government guaranteed constancy. A guaranteed value is neither necessary nor possible. All that is necessary is that those who print paper claims against gold specify the quantity of gold their paper claims represent, and that they adhere to their promise to pay by not undermining their ability to convert their claims into gold—that is, they do not fraudulently increase their note issuance. The result would be a mild fluctuation of gold in relation to other commodities and monies.

Further, to advocate pegging gold to a given number of dollars would only amount to a fiction in today's inflationary climate, just as it would be a fiction to fix the price of any commodity. The free market must be allowed to determine the value of gold and all money substitutes, just as it determines the value of any and all commodities—by supply, consumer demand, and the cost of production. Just as there is no validity to the case for price controls, there is no validity to the case for exchange controls.

If people want security of purchasing power, they need not and should not look for government guaranteed security; they can easily obtain security through the free market by including in all contracts that purchases, repayments, and the like be made in money adjusted to compensate for any changes in the value of money. Futures markets can be, and have been, established in any commodity, money, or money substitute that individuals show a desire to participate in. Yet rarely have most people sought a guaranteed protection against loss.

Those who argue for an official price of gold can only hurt the case for a free market and therefore a gold standard. Price controls contradict a free market and therefore should be avoided. This includes control of all prices, including the price of money. Price controls have always been counterproductive and self-defeating. Worse, they establish the principle of government-provided security at the expense of individual freedom. To argue that an official price of gold is necessary and desirable is to argue that the free market is not.

The Devaluation Syndrome

The argument that there must be and/or should be a major devaluation of the dollar is an offshoot of the official price argument. It accepts all the premises of that argument and therefore makes the same mistakes. But there are further implications of this argument that must be examined.

First, devaluation means a return to a monetary system of fixed exchange rates at a time when inflation makes it impossible to fix the value of anything, let alone the value of money. Bretton Woods is an eloquent example of what happens, given fixed exchange rates together with inflationary policies. It is not good enough to say, "Well, we shouldn't have inflation. Fixed exchange rates would work if government stopped printing money and adhered to the value of the monetary unit." The fact is that we do have inflation and may continue to have inflation for many years to come. The devaluation argument drops the matter out of context and reverses cause and effect by demanding a system of stable money and prices at a time when there is no reason to assume that this kind of stability is possible to the world at this time.

Second, the devaluation argument delegates to the International Monetary Fund the power to establish an international monetary system by law. Implicit in the devaluation argument is acceptance of the unfounded assumption offered by the IMF, that this time the devaluation and exchange rate realignment will be final. Many advocates of a gold standard unwittingly accept this assumption and thus believe that the way to achieve a gold standard is through a major devaluation, which would reestablish a convertible gold dollar. This, they believe, is the way to eliminate inflation.

But, in fact, just the opposite is true. It is not a gold standard that will lead to the elimination of inflation; it is the elimination of inflation that will lead to a gold standard. To attempt to maintain an international gold standard through the IMF is impossible, given today's political context—we would only end up going off gold again, with gold getting the blame for the resulting crisis. Allow individual gold ownership and use of gold as money and an international gold standard will naturally evolve—when and only when government monetary policy becomes noninflationary. Until then, gold and exchange rates of national monies should be left free to seek their own levels.

Fixed exchange rates will never (and should never) result from a formal international organization such as the IMF. The stability of exchange rates will be the result not of government price fixing, but of noninflationary adherence to the value of money—the elimination of legal sanctions that permit any government agency or bank to fraudulently increase the money supply.

Under a gold standard in which all nations deal in weights of gold, exchange rates would necessarily be fixed by relative weight—not by law. No formal international monetary system would be necessary and no nation would be forced into, or prevented from, using other monies such as silver, paper, and so forth. A gold standard does not require exchange rates fixed by law. It assumes only that exchange rates will be fixed as a result of adherence to the definition of money. This means that if a monetary unit is defined as one ounce of gold, it will necessarily exchange for other monetary units at a precise ratio—unless the monetary unit is debased and misrepresented.

Thus there is no need for a formal, legal, international monetary system. All that is needed is the free market. The way back to a gold standard is not backward toward the Bretton Woods system, but forward toward a noninflationary system of freely self-adjusting exchange rates in terms of currencies and gold.

Third, the argument for devaluation is inconsistent with and contradicts another main argument propagated today by gold advocates: The world is headed for runaway inflation and/or depression and deflation. If it can be reasonably assumed that prices may skyrocket or plunge, as most gold advocates contend, what sense does it make to advocate raising the price of gold and fixing exchange rates? If it is anticipated that prices will fluctuate dramatically, exchange rates need to be as flexible as possible to adjust quickly to people's changing economic evaluations, to price/cost factors, and to supply and demand conditions. It makes no sense at all to advocate fixing the price of gold, exchange rates (or anything else) when expectations are that prices will rise or fall dramatically. Such price controls are doomed to failure and can only result in dangerous economic and monetary distortions that will ultimately lead to the restriction of trade and to a lower standard of living for individuals.

The Stop Printing Money Argument

Inflation is the fraudulent increase in the supply of money and credit. It is both immoral and impractical to inflate. Eventually inflation might be outlawed, but not today—and not overnight. Both rational economic analysis and history verify the disastrous consequences possible given a dramatic increase or decrease in a nation's money stock.

In today's context, when the whole of the American banking system and economy is geared toward inflationary finance, it is to no one's short-term or long-term interest to advocate that government should immediately stop printing money or that the inflationary arm of government—the Federal Reserve Board—should be abolished. For, taken literally, these well-meaning intentions could result in a nightmare of economic turmoil.

Rather, it should be stressed that the supply of fiat money should be slowly reduced and stabilized to correspond to increases in the gold supply, and that structural changes within the banking system should take place to facilitate elimination of the artificial and arbitrary nature of note issuance. This would reduce inflation and go a long way toward establishing the proper direction necessary for a return to gold.

The case against inflation can never be stated too often and its importance to a sound monetary system can never be overemphasized. Clearly the battle against inflation must be won before the return to a gold standard can be secure. But neither can the importance and necessity of a gradual return to gold be overemphasized.

Inflation certainly is immoral and economically impractical—but so is any proposal that aims to unleash unnecessary hardship on citizens in the name of morality and practicality. The road back to a gold standard will be long and hard, but the road should be made as smooth as possible by intelligent guidance. Thus, advocates of a return to the gold standard should make clear their intentions. They advocate a reduction in the fraudulent increase of the money supply—which means a reduction to the point at which this increase is based on the production of a particular commodity—which means gradual departure from a government-regulated money supply and gradual return to a market-regulated money supply.

The Demonetization Threat

To demonetize usually means to remove a particular form of money from circulation. In this sense, gold has been demonetized

in the United States for years. But this is not what many opponents of gold mean when they say gold should be demonetized.
They believe that, internationally, the official role of gold should
be reduced and finally eliminated among governments and that,
nationally, gold should circulate like any other commodity. Gold
advocates usually denounce this intent to demonetize as an
attempt to undermine the principle of the gold standard in order
to more effectively pursue inflationary policies. This certainly may
be the intention, but in today's context demonetization could be a
very good thing for gold advocates and a very bad thing for the
opponents of gold. Consider the following facts:

- Gold cannot by itself prevent inflation. If policy makers are
  determined to inflate, they will do so with or without gold.
  For the most part, the degree of inflation will depend on the
  lack of knowledge or irrationality of policy makers and can
  only be combated by the knowledge and rationality of a
  nation's citizens.
- Gold is primarily used by governments to give an unwarranted
  status and credibility to their fiat money—a status and credibility that could not be maintained if gold is demonetized and
  allowed to circulate alongside the depreciating money of
  government.
- If it is true that today's governments are notoriously poor
  money managers, why entrust them with the majority of the
  world's gold? Would it not be put to better use managed by
  individuals?

The road back to a gold standard is an educational one; it
may take us as many decades to return to gold as it took to
abandon it. With governments as the major holders of gold in the

world today, citizens derive little or none of the benefits of gold. This prevents the kind of self-education that might occur given popular exposure to gold. Rather than campaigning against demonetization of gold or for legal tender gold legislation, gold advocates should seek repeal of legal tender restrictions on the use of gold in payment of private debts.

In today's context, demonetization means to return gold to individuals. At a time when all the evidence points to the mismanagement of gold by governments, when it is plain that governments are using gold to their citizens' disadvantage, when there is no reason to assume that policy makers desire or even know how to return to a gold standard, why advocate a government program to return to gold? Government will be the last to realize the virtue and importance of gold as money.

Gold has no business being in the possession of such so-called money managers. Let governments have their fiat money and receive the full responsibility and blame for their note depreciation; let individuals regain governments' gold and rediscover the benefits of gold; make the policy makers' phrase, "gold is a barbarous relic," a government position; let both gold and fiat money circulate among individuals and we'll then see who possesses, determines, and controls money—individuals or governments.

On Context, Cause, and Effect

It is important that one recognize just how far the educational process of this country must go before a return to the gold standard is possible. The gold standard requires monetary stability, which means that the majority of U.S. citizens must oppose all those government domestic programs now popularly advocated and financed through inflation. Further, a gold standard requires economic stability, which means all of the malinvestments, overconsumption, and misallocation of resources that have resulted from years of artificial, government-made booms and led to a multitude of economic distortions must take their toll. This means that the anticipation of recessions, depressions, inflation, or deflation must be behind Americans and the reasonable expectations of economic stability and real growth established for a period of time. This kind of stability is a long way off—yet this is the kind of stability necessary before a gold standard can be established as a lasting monetary system. The gold standard could never last long without confidence in future monetary and economic stability. If those presently advocating gold ownership and the ownership of other investment hedges are doing so because they are convinced that the world is headed for great monetary and economic instability, they should be equally convinced that it still is far too soon to be advocating a full return to the gold standard.

Even more premature is the attempt to submit specific proposals of exactly how to return to the gold standard. This problem must be seen in context. Even assuming that people desire to return to gold, any specific plans for implementing a return to gold will depend greatly on such factors as international monetary arrangements and conditions, domestic monetary and economic conditions, and the legal, financial, and structural conditions of the banking system. These conditions change. Thus, a good proposal today may be sadly lacking a year from now. Until fundamental political changes occur in this country, it is unreasonable for anyone to assume they must address themselves to the question of specifically how to return to a gold standard.

Rather, they should concern themselves with eliminating those laws that are preventing them from using gold as money and attacking those policies that encourage government inflation. The

143

legalization of gold and its use as money, an end to legal tender laws, the freedom of individuals to mint coins, and the elimination of laws that prevent banks from existing independently of the Federal Reserve System—all these are valid interim measures one can advocate. But the problem of how to return to a gold standard will be solved, for the most part, through solving more fundamental problems.

A full gold standard cannot return until economic stability returns; we cannot return to economic stability until we return to monetary stability. Monetary stability cannot be secured until the source, nature, and immorality of inflation is exposed to and understood by Americans. But the evils of inflation cannot be understood until individuals grasp the meaning of money and the nature of property rights. And property rights will not be secured without a full understanding and defense of individual rights. Thus, nothing less than a return to laissez faire capitalism and a free market will insure a return to and defense of the gold standard. Therefore, a massive and extensive educational task on the virtues of capitalism confronts all those who desire to effectively fight for a gold standard.

People will want to return to gold only when they rediscover what money is, and people will not rediscover what money is until they understand why what they have is not money.

Part IV

INVESTING IN GOLD

Chapter 12

Lessons of a Life-Long Gold Investor

The task of a successful investor is twofold: To have a general view of the future and to understand that the odds of being right about the future are, shall we say, precarious at best. If we were gurus and psychics we wouldn't have to bother with such things as theories or prognostications. But as long as there are the possibilities of inflation and deflation, booms and busts, and bubbles, panics, and crises, we are forced to try and become forecasters of the economy.

There are as many methods of making money as there are investors. In fact, when it comes right down to it, all investing is individual in nature. A lot of people don't believe that knowledge about the economy is important. Those that are only interested in the value and prospects of a particular company look at company fundamentals and are less concerned about the state of the economy. Yet, we know that for the most part, when there are booms or panics, all stocks tend to rise and fall together. They say, "A rising tide lifts all boats." True. And it is also true that all boats are battered by hurricanes. The dot-com craze and the market crash of 2009 are examples of how mass psychology can lead to massive profits and losses.

Chartists also don't care much for economic knowledge. They believe that the movements of stocks themselves carry all the knowledge one needs to make decisions on investing. Since human action is what moves markets, why try to decipher what people think about the world when you can simply track the actions they take? Chartists believe that the market has innate information and all that is known is in the market or a stock at any one time. It's a fair point. The market reflects human values and human action. But then how do you explain a stock falling out of bed on bad news? Or the market crashing after 9/11? Where was the innate knowledge beforehand?

Personally, I am not a chartist, but I respect them and follow them. Charts provide context. Since a large percent of the investment community are chartists, I am always aware of technical support and resistance levels, and the trends indicated by moving averages. It makes little sense to stand in the way of a major breakout or breakdown of charts and the stampede that usually follows if you are a trader. As an investor, it matters little. Over time the fundamentals always prevail.

One way to narrow the risk of being wrong about an investment is to specialize. I have chosen gold, including other resources such as silver and copper, as my main focus. The gold market is a very savvy market. To play in it, you need a thorough knowledge of things like the causes of inflation and deflation; the determinants and effects of changing interest rates and exchange rates; the influence of government policy on markets, money, and the economy; the causes of recessions, and what separates a boom from a bubble. Without such knowledge you may do okay, but you will not be in front of the market; you will be following it. Being in front is where the big money is made.

The chapters in this book give you the information needed to put the world of economics into context. History, cause and effect, interest rate growth, money supply growth, the movement in exchange rates, trade policy, acts of government intervention, all affect interest rates, stocks, and commodities. The information in this book can be important to people for different reasons—political, educational, historical, or personal. But it is very important to those that want to invest in or trade the precious metals market. One new piece of information that breaks and is interpreted properly can make your year.

Let me tell you a story.

One moonless night, in a community nestled in a valley, the electricity provided by the one and only power company ceased. All of the lights in the valley went off. By candlelight, the manager of the plant found the name of the plant's architect and sent for him by messenger.

Soon the architect showed up with a small briefcase. He asked the manager if he had the original plans. With some fuss he found them and gave them to the architect who immediately inspected them. "Take me to tunnel three," he said. They walked for some time and finally arrived at tunnel three. Overhead were rows of large pipes. The architect opened his case and took out a small hammer. He tapped on one of the pipes three times. Immediately all of the lights in the valley lit up.

The manager was elated. He praised the architect for his efficiency and told him to send him a bill. Three days later the manager received a bill for $25,000.75. The manager was shocked. He finally called the architect and asked, "How did you arrive at a figure of 25 grand? And what in the heck is the 75 cents for!"

The architect replied "Sir. The 75 cents was for the three taps in which I only charged you 25 cents a tap. The $25,000 is for knowing *where* to tap."

The moral of the story? It's a knowledge-based world. Knowledge is the best creator and protector of wealth.

There are very successful investors and traders who vary greatly in their approaches. At the end of the day it is success over time that will determine one's ability to be a full-time investor. I place great weight on fundamentals, which means I rely on knowledge and my ability to identify the emergence of new factors that will affect the economy, project the direction of the economy, and recognize turns in the economy. There are excellent chartists, and very good stock pickers. I am not one of them. I have survived by my ability to quickly and correctly identify the facts of reality, form them into a theory, and then integrate the information into a new view of the world, or at least a view of a newly arising situation. The key is to be nimble enough to beat others to the correct trade on this knowledge.

Which reminds me of another story.

Two young executives were driving in the wilderness and mountains of Oregon. Their BMW stopped cold on a lonely highway. After many attempts to get the car started again, they tried phoning the auto club. But no service was available. So they both grabbed their attaché cases and started walking back down the road when all of a sudden a huge grizzly bear roared. They turned and saw it standing on its hind legs silhouetted by the full moon. It fell on all fours and started to run towards them.

Both execs took off running and as they looked back they saw the bear gaining on them. All of a sudden one of them stopped, kneeled down, opened up his attaché case, and took out a pair of Nike running shoes and started to slip them on.

The other exec, huffing and puffing, looked at him and said, "You're not going to be able to beat that bear with those." The exec finished tying his shoes looked up and said, "I don't have to beat the bear. I just have to beat you!"

This goes a long way in describing the art of trading and speculation in markets. Speed and timing is everything. Stay ahead of the other players and your chances of a successful outcome improve exponentially. Today, with flash trading and black boxes running trades at 2,000 per second, you'd think you would be at a disadvantage as a trader. But remember, computers don't think. You need to get out of their way at times, but you can beat them anytime they are wrong. And there are times when they will be wrong and you will be right. The key to success is knowing the difference.

On Trading

I remember an incident in 1968. I was just starting my investment career and was at my broker's. Back then that was the only place you could get instant information. Back then we "read the tape" and followed our stocks and commodities on Quotron machines. Quotron machines were invented not long after beads and rattles were introduced into the medical profession.

A Quotron machine looked like a slot machine. The quotes were where the cherries or flaming sevens would be. Silver was trading at around $1.50 and I was long the silver market, looking for $5. Johnson Matthey, the biggest silver trading company on the street, came out with the statement that there was enough silver available above ground to last 100 years. All of a sudden my Quotron machine looked like a one-armed bandit whose lever had just been pulled. By the time I could get out of my silver position, silver had plunged to $1.29. As Groucho Marx once quipped about the crash of 1929, "I saw a fortune wiped out in a twinkling of an eye." It was then that I realized that I needed to start putting in protective stops. Live and learn!

By the end of the decade of the 1970s, the Hunt Brothers were attempting to corner the silver market. Silver soared to over $50 an ounce. The government moved in and literally prevented traders from going long silver by preventing the buying of silver futures contracts. If you can't buy and only sell, you must sell. The price of silver crashed and the Hunt Brothers, along with everyone else long silver, got wiped out. This is the power of government, and it should never be underestimated. Protective stops—either mental or physical—allow you to protect yourself against both market forces and the force of government, and I might add, your own preconceived notions.

The Rules of the Game

Even with a sophisticated understanding of economic and monetary policy, there is no guarantee that you will make money. On the contrary, some of the best economists that ever lived could never turn their knowledge into profits. It takes a knack to make money over the long term. When people ask me what method I use to play the market I usually reply, "The seat of my pants method." I am only half kidding. In bridge, the greatest card game in the world, there is a phrase, "feel of the board." It refers to the person playing the hand being able to get a sense of where all the other cards are around him, mentally place them, then devise a plan of attack and attempt to make the contract and win the game. It has much to do with strategy, but it also has to do with informed intuition. It is this that allows me to enter or retreat from a position successfully. It comes from both knowledge and experience. I don't know how many times I've felt like I've been here before and sensed the need to exit or enter a position because of it.

'On any day, in any week, or any month, I may pick more stock losers than winners. What keeps me in the game, as a trader, is knowledge, informed intuition, and rules. The first rule, as far as I am concerned, is "Cut losses quickly and let profits run." This rule allows me to be wrong more times than I am right, yet in the long term, make money. I can have five small losses but two or three good runs in a stock or a commodity, and that puts me ahead of the game at the end of the year.

Now, I trust my knowledge, and I am willing to rely on my experience, but not to the point of risking my life's savings on them. I trust no one to be right about the direction of the market or a stock— including myself. I have learned to never fall in love with a stock or a commodity or buck a market trend. Never find yourself in a position of having to explain why you are right and the market is wrong. You will not survive for long as an investor or a trader if you do.

You must never be in the position of proclaiming "the market is irrational." It doesn't matter whether it is or it isn't! What matters is whether you make money or lose money. Every trade should be based on fresh fundamentals and accompanied by either mental or physical stops. Stops are your protection against yourself. It limits your mistakes and thereby limits what you can lose. Cut losses, let profits run.

When to Be Flexible . . .

I am not a gold bug. Gold bugs have a position in gold come hell or high water. To short gold is blasphemy. Gold is like a religion to gold bugs. They are perma bulls. At the time of this writing the price of gold is about $1,400. If for any reason the price begins to fall, the downside can be huge. Knowing this, I have already devised my strategy of how to short gold if necessary. I have learned never to fall in love with a position. I am not wedded to gold, except as an insurance policy. So, if and when the bull market ends in gold, I expect to be one of the first out with the profits this bull market has provided.

I have very strong beliefs in the efficacy of free markets. I trust that gold will rise over time in an inflationary economy. Yet, like I've said, I will not hesitate to short gold, or the market, or stocks that I like if I think it is warranted. Economics is not a religion. Likewise, there is no conservative economics or liberal economics. There is simply economics! It is a social science dependent on the values and actions of individuals. Those values and actions can be rational or irrational. My job is to make money off of either.

Another rule I go by is that fundamentals trump technicals. The gold market is basically a fundamentalist market at its core. For example, if the Fed suddenly announced it was going to dramatically increase the money supply, gold would soar. If they announced they were going to raise interest rates in the disinflationary recessionary-prone economy, gold would plunge. Technicals are important; however, they are more important in the absence of

154

news. They give traders a context in which to trade. But the news itself, particularly breaking news, is what will drive markets—up and down.

Trading means just that. It means changing positions. Traders are agnostics when it comes to monetary or political theories. Traders try to get in front of a trend and ride it as far as it will take them until the market stops them out. There are, however exceptions to rules. There are always exceptions. One should never put stops on a stock that is thinly traded. That will only insure that you will get the worse possible fill. If you sell into a falling market you are likely to push the market lower if there is low volume. You will be playing against yourself. It's better to maintain a mental stop and try and sell manually, and if possible always try to sell into a rising market and buy into a falling one. Thin markets are dangerous and not usually conducive to trading. Buy and hold is the best policy when playing thinly traded stocks.

The same difficulty exists on the upside. If there is one thing that I've learned about bull markets, it's when they take off they tend not to let you in. I can't tell you how many times I've watched a stock shoot up and waited for a reasonable pullback just to see the stock double and redouble again. There is nothing reasonable about a roaring bull market.

Some can last for years, such as the dot-com bull market of the 1990s or the gold run of the twenty-first century. Apple computer's stellar performance is another example. The best way to enter a bull run on a stock is to just buy it. Averaging the price, by buying it if it goes down from your entry point, or up, is another good tactic. Then tuck it away and live with it. When the momentum has ended, then you can decide whether or not to keep the stock or sell it.

Never look at your purchase price for a stock to determine whether it's a good sell (or a good buy). Always look at the facts at the time, not the history. The least important piece of information, as to your decision to buy or sell, is the price history of a stock and your cost basis. Always look at the prospects for profits based on the value of a stock and your expectations of performance going forward at the time.

. . . And When to Stick to Your Guns

The other exception to a rule is when you have extreme confidence in the long-term direction of a market or company. In the 1970s the stock market was pretty much dead. Gold had been fixed for 30 years. There were few gold-producing companies able to survive back then. Homestake Mining was one of the few. Only a handful of investors were focused on the fate of the dollar and the potential for gold back then. In 1968, *Death of the Dollar* by William F. Rickenbacker was published and alerted its readers to the very real possibility of a future devaluation of the dollar against gold.

In 1970, Harry Browne wrote *How You Can Profit from the Coming Devaluation*. I myself wrote the articles "The Making of an International Monetary Crisis" and "The Death of Bretton Woods," warning of inflation, further devaluations of currencies, and the importance of gold in the monetary system—and gold and silver stocks in one's portfolio. In 1971, Nixon devalued the dollar, and in 1975 gold was legalized and American citizens allowed to acquire and invest in it.

During those years gold soared from $35 an ounce to over $100. Stocks like Homestake Mining soared together with many others, especially South African gold stocks. Yet, after a good run they began to fall again. As the Fed began to raise interest rates and tighten money, recession set in and all markets fell, including gold and gold stocks.

Knowing that the increase in the price of gold was not a fluke or a fad, and that the inflationary policies of government had not changed, I did not sell my entire position in gold stocks, although I took profits. Sometimes holding a core position in stocks is the best course. As the price fell I began to average into more shares and build an even larger position.

By 1980 gold soared past $800 and I cashed out my position. Stops are advisable for trading but buying on dips and averaging your price downward in a falling market can sometimes be the best tactic as long as you are in a long-term bull market. Rule: Buy low, sell high. Averaging can be the best way to make a huge profit—as long as you are right on the ultimate direction. Remember, whether trading or investing, look to maximize profits but only put up what you can afford to lose. Losses come with the territory. Count on them.

On Investing

The year 1980 was an inflection point in many markets. It was the end of the bull market in gold. And although the bull market in common stocks would not begin until 1982, the seeds were being sown that year for the greatest bull market in stocks in history.

In November 1980, Ronald Reagan was elected President of the United States. Unless you lived through the 1960s and 1970s you cannot understand the level of cynicism and anticapitalistic sentiment this country was mired in. It was a time of war, when our policy was to fight a sacrificial war of dubious national interest, with tactics that prevented our soldiers from winning. Body bags were being sent home by the hundreds weekly, riots were a normal event in U.S. streets. University campuses were being burned, and assassination of our nation's leaders was not uncommon. Economic and political turmoil was the norm for two decades.

Communism, fascism, and socialism, which together spell "statism," were in vogue and openly being taught in our universities of higher learning. Government intervention was, politically, standard operating procedure. Such was the state of the union back then. We had three recessions in 10 years, inflation that rose progressively for two decades, unemployment that went above 10 percent, an oil shock, the imposition of wage and price controls resulting in rationing, which led to shortages and long lines at gas stations, a crashing dollar, an anticapitalism mentality in and out of government, and a stock market that was stagnant for a decade.

It was in this environment that a handful of intellectuals spoke out. Ayn Rand, author of *Atlas Shrugged*, challenged the world's philosophy, morals, and economic and political beliefs. She wrote *Capitalism: The Unknown Ideal* at the height of the statist revolution. Milton Friedman also challenged the establishment. He wrote several books on the dollar, deficits, capitalism, and freedom, which began to move the country back toward free market economics. Between Ayn Rand's philosophical movement and Friedman's economic movement the country began to look at alternative political and economic policies.

Ideas move the world. The ideas of freedom slowly worked their way back into the universities of America and into the minds of some academics. An intellectual battle was in progress. The last link in the chain is always politics. And after two decades of ruinous policies, America was due for a rebirth.

Ronald Reagan had been governor of California, and after his eight-year term ended he began doing a weekly commentary on the radio. He talked economics and politics for over two years. It became obvious that he had a broad understanding of classical economics, a deep trust of freedom and free markets, and mistrust of government intervention. He was one of the few eloquent voices that championed freedom and free market economics during the seventies. Reagan won his run for the presidency by a landslide and, slowly, markets began to repair themselves.

In August 1982, the birth of the longest and strongest bull market in history began. It was in that month that I, as an investment advisor, wrote a letter and sent it to everyone I knew who was involved in investing. I advised selling all gold stocks— many that were up 10 to 20 times in value—and switching the money to common stocks. I stated that I thought the market could triple by the end of the decade and that we were in for what I called a "technological revolution" that, like the industrial revolution, could last 20 to 30 years.

That view was considered wildly optimistic and I received not one interested response. No one believed the country could be repaired.

When investing, you want to establish a position for the long term. You assume that over many years this investment will grow. This is true in a gold bull market or a common stock bull market. They say not to put all of your eggs in one basket. I disagree. I have always put all of my eggs in one basket and have been doing so for over four decades. While I held my physical gold as an insurance policy, I bought a basket of diverse technology stocks that I felt were poised to lead the technological revolution I envisioned. The Dow was 776 when I entered the market. By

1990 it was approaching 3,000. For those of you who are not able or interested in trading, investing can be just as profitable. The key is to wait for a major turn of events, take a position, and hold. Or simply ride a trend in progress and add to your position if you can.

Shakeouts

Whether a trader or an investor, you will run across the inevitable shakeout. In 1987, the market was in a major boom. From out of nowhere the stock market crashed. It crashed in October 1987 to a greater degree than even the crash of 1929. I was completely out of the market and on the sidelines on that Black Monday. I did not like what I was hearing from the Secretary of the Treasury regarding a return to a possible cheap dollar policy. A reversal in the dollar would raise interest rates and crater the stock market.

The fear of just such a possibility threw fear into the market and investors ran for the exits. The crash was exacerbated by program trading and derivative trading aided by leverage, much like the crashes recently. Many investors never entered the market again after that day. Yet there was no recession as a result of the greatest crash in history. I reentered the market on the basis that the fundamental policies that led us out of the greatest recession since the Great Depression were still in play and that there was no structural damage to the economy due to the crash.

In fact the Administration immediately reaffirmed its strong dollar policy and its determination to "stay the course" and the markets returned to normal. Unfortunately at any time a government action or statement can move markets dramatically. During the seventies and early eighties, I used to wait up until the 12 A.M. radio news broadcast, where, if I was lucky, they would quote the Hong Kong gold price. Many times in the era of fixed exchange rates, there would be midnight devaluations. The world would wake up the next day and find that the German mark or the French franc had been devalued by 10 percent. You learned to know devaluation was imminent because of the constant government denials that would precede it.

I remember being in the gold market as the Treasury announced they would begin selling gold to defend the dollar and the gold market fell out of bed. I was in the market when the leading gold-holding nations announced they were to embark on a five-year selling program. Again, gold tanked. Both times I was stopped out of my position. Many times, before and since, I was shaken out of my position but forced to buy back in at higher prices.

Shakeouts, for whatever reason, and regardless of cause, force you out of a position. Invariably the stock you're in returns to its previous level and moves up from there.

I have been shaken out of stocks and markets more times than I'd care to admit, but I always recouped quickly. One reason I do is that I don't look back. Always start each new trade or position fresh. Look at the fundamentals and the value of the stock you want, and if it makes sense to invest, make your move. There is nothing to gain by dwelling on past losses or the injustice of the market. Look forward and continue to do what has been working. And try to avoid the next shakeout . . . because it's coming.

I've also had my share of spotting potential shakeouts and avoiding them. I managed to avoid the bear market in gold that began in 1980 and switched to common stocks, and I avoided the crash of 1987. Perhaps the best sidestepping of a market reversal was my last. In July 2007, just before the financial crisis began, I wrote an article called "You Never See the Snake That Bites You." In it I said the following:

. . . as an investor I am always looking at the message of the market on a minute-to-minute, hour-to-hour basis. Just like a weatherman, this is what I do. Today (July 20th, 2007), I saw something I haven't seen in a very long time. For a few minutes there was a whiff of crisis in the air. In a period of about five minutes the stock market fell from down about 100 points to over 200 points, the bond market rallied as the 10-year interest rate fell from 5.01 percent to 4.94 percent, while at the same time non-government paper *rose* in yield (very unusual) and gold rose from up 2 dollars to up 10 dollars. Just as a weatherman takes heed of dark clouds forming, I started looking for snakes.

What would cause this unusual combination of market responses? There are a lot of snakes in the bushes out there, but the market knows about most of them. The market knows about inflation and signals it through higher gold prices, but a rising bond market contradicts that possibility.

The market knows about the credit concerns and has discounted suspect paper by raising the risk premium on most nongovernment, nonguaranteed paper. And it knows about the housing slump, derivatives, and hedge fund worries. It's all out there.

But there may be a snake lurking that the market has not got a glimpse of yet. There are rumors that a sub prime fund in Australia and two sub prime funds in England are in trouble. Most Americans think the housing boom was an American phenomenon, but it was worldwide. If the stock market continues down, which I suggested shorting Thursday, and if a fund or two folds, and if a few buyout deals can't be financed next week, at the same time as the housing numbers come out, which should be lousy, we could have the makings of a reinstatement of the recessionary–disinflationary bias of years ago.

Now, what happened today may be a ripple that in the scheme of things will disappear next week, but on the other hand I'm always on the lookout for that snake I don't see.

Once again, knowledge and the ability to integrate it into a new view of the world saved me the anguish of most other investors. While 95 percent lost money in 2008–2009, I had two of the best years in my career.

Turning a Disadvantage into an Advantage

But it's not always that way. Inevitably you are going to zig when you should zag and you will find yourself in a world of hurt. I ended up reentering the gold market in the late 1990s as gold fell from the 500 level to under 350. I was premature in taking a position in gold that year, but the idea that gold could fall another hundred dollars seemed remote.

I sat there for almost three years and watched the value of my gold stocks dwindle away as it did just that. I did three things that turned that miserable experience into an opportunity.

First, as the market declined prior to 2001, I averaged my position. At the bottom of the market I had accumulated thousands of shares versus hundreds of shares as my dollar stocks turned into penny stocks. So, when the bull market arrived, I had a position in gold stocks that I would never been able to afford without the occurrence of the bear market.

Second, Congress passed a law allowing investors to convert their IRAs into Roth IRAs, which if you paid the taxes owed on the account you could avoid any income taxes on the distributed proceeds or the profits forever! I immediately called my broker and converted. My gold stocks had fallen substantially in that account as gold fell to the "impossible" level of $250 an ounce. The taxes I paid were insignificant. As the gold market rallied in 2001 I eventually turned that IRA account into a 10-bagger, tax free!

And finally, when gold stocks became so cheap as to defy reality, I margined those stocks that I could in my margin account. I continued to add to my margin account all the way up and finally liquidated it in 2002. It turned out that the taxes I ended up paying on my margin account equaled more than the dollar amount of my original position when I began the accumulation.

Always try to look for the opportunities when things go against you. Taking a disadvantage and turning it to an advantage can be one of the most rewarding things you ever do.

On Leverage

I mentioned the use of margin above. I am not opposed to leverage, but it needs to be monitored closely. Obviously if you buy a stock that doubles you will make much more profit if you have two or three times the amount of stock than not, but you will also lose two or three times as much if the stock drops. There is a time for leverage and a time not to touch it. There have been times when I have used margin and made substantially more than I otherwise would. And there were times I used options, which provided even more leverage. But what intrigues me today are exchange traded funds, ETFs.

ETFs are new structured derivatives that try to allow the individual investors to diversify by buying a basket of stocks or commodities, or playing various sectors of the economy. You can buy gold through an ETF without taking possession or having to store it. Or you can go long the Standard & Poor's 500 or NASDAQ. You can take a position in Real Estate Investment Trusts (REITs) or commodities like natural gas or agriculture. Or play either large banks or just regional banks if you wish.

Thousands of ETFs have been created over the last few years. You can go long or short with an ETF. You can buy an ETF (or an inverse ETF) that tracks a group of stocks or commodities at twice the underlying basket's movement—or even three times its movement. And you can do this in your IRA where, until ETFs were invented, you were prohibited from going short or buying on margin.

It is a testimony to the impotence of government regulations that at the height of the complaints against unregulated derivatives we have had the greatest explosion of derivatives to date. And to further illustrate the point, they are allowed to bypass the regulations on margin and short sales in IRAs. (I would not be surprised to see some ETFs regulated or even outlawed in the future, certainly in IRAs, which would be much to my disappointment.)

I have to tell you, I love the invention of ETFs. I am not a stock picker. I'm a theorist. So the invention of ETFs that allow me to play commodities, bonds, and economic sectors from the long or short side is a gift! To allow me to have the choice of buying into a diversified basket that moves two and three times normal is a double and triple gift. Yet with every gift comes a curse.

ETFs are prone to program trading. This means that they are more irrational and more volatile. Black boxes buy and sell at preprogrammed trigger points in nanoseconds. They can push or pull markets dramatically faster than humans can. The flash crash in May of 2010 was a modern day, high-tech, repeat of the crash of 1987—that was also caused by program trading. We live in a more challenging world than ever, and I am sure we have just seen a sample of things to come.

Flash trading is replacing human judgment. It is certainly beating it daily. We live in a brave new world and it is not stopping for anyone nor is it controllable or predictable. The common thread running through this new form of trading is that it tends to create extreme volatility. It runs stops and virtually wipes them out.

The flash crash was a great example of this. Once the market broke technical support it fell a thousand points in ten minutes. By the end of the day it was as if nothing happened except a bad day in the market, as we recouped most all of the loss. But everyone with defensive sell stops in place was removed from the market. The black boxes, in effect, ran the table.

Let me tell you a story of what happened to me that particular day. I had a buy stop in as a strategy to take advantage of a falling market. My plan was to take an initial position in TZA, an ETF that is triple short the market, at seven. If it moved to six I'd reenter the market. If it moved to eight, I'd buy more. I placed a sell stop just under my initial position at 6.75. The market dropped like a rock, TZA soared, and I bought it at eight (something I expected to happen in about a month from then, not in the next 10 minutes). Then the market rallied and I was stopped out of my original position!

Consider it: We had one of the biggest market drops on record, I was short, and I was sitting in a loss position! Do you know what the odds are for something like that happening?

Lesson: If and when things start going against you consistently and you cannot figure out why, take a time-out. Pull your short-term money and stop trading and reevaluate. Remember, we now live in the world of the machines and we are in unknown territory.

When to Sell a Stock

There's an old expression, "Some people just can't stand prosperity." This is particularly true of those of us who play the market. It always seems easier to endure a bear market than to ride a bull market to its conclusion. In a bear market we simply hold to our convictions and are sustained by our dreams of eventual wealth. But in a bull market we are torn between greed and fear.

Bull markets are always much more mentally taxing. On the one hand, we want to catch the very highs and make the maximum profit. But on the other hand, we never want to be out of the market, lest we look like fools, leaving a load of money on the table.

The obvious time to sell out a position is when there is a clear change of policy from better to worse, or worse to better, or an event that significantly changes the investment climate. Once again knowledge is key. How you interpret events is where the big money is.

Notwithstanding an event, I have always found that there are certain benchmarks that help one make it easier to know when to sell. When there is maximum euphoria and you're sure we are going much higher and stocks spike upward, that's usually a good time to sell. Another is to sell when you reach a personal financial goal. This way, no matter what happens, you have attained a personal value. If you make a personal target that you believe is reasonable at the time you take a position and sell when that objective is met, then don't look back. Take the money and declare victory.

Another good rule is to sell half your position every time you double your money. There's an old adage, "Bulls make money, bears make money, but pigs get slaughtered." Learning how to accept prosperity is always harder than it seems. It usually has nothing to do with how things look at the time, since highs are made when you are absolutely sure the market is going higher—and doesn't. Similarly, lows are made when you're nauseous and about to throw up on your shoes.

One more strategy for taking profits seems to work. Let the market take you out. Follow the bull run with trailing stops. When you are stopped out, stay stopped out. You may not make the max, but you'll never lose much, either. And if the market exceeds your expectations, you'll be in longer and make more money than you expected.

All of these methods are effective, but in the last analysis, we all have to learn to live with our decisions. Whether profit or loss, there is always going to be another profit opportunity in the future. So, whenever you take a profit, enjoy it—and for God's sake try not to give it back.

"Be Afraid. Be Very, Very, Afraid . . ."

Because of the extreme volatility of markets, you can be doing everything right and still have your head handed to you in an instant. Not only do we have the fastest computers known to humans to contend with as individual investors, we have government intervention to deal with. No matter how hard government tries to protect us—or control us—government regulations will not end crises, panics, and recessions.

The possibilities of what can go wrong and the theoretical scenarios from booms to busts are endless:

- The government will reach a point where it can no longer service its debt. Bondholders will dump their bonds and interest rates will soar to over 20 percent, throwing the economy into depression.

- Taxes rise, interest rates rise, the economy slows, unemployment goes up, and defaults on credit card debt, home mortgages, and home equity loans soar. Home prices spiral downward, affecting all other prices. Deflation and a Japan-style deflationary depression take hold and send us into decades of stagnation.

- As it becomes obvious to the rest of the world that the United States cannot pay its debts, foreign holders of dollars panic and begin to dump them. The dollar falls but as it becomes obvious that no nation can pay its debts and that all are at risk, there develops a flight out of all paper money and paper substitutes such as bonds and currencies. This leads to the breakdown of the international monetary system, hyperinflation, and the wiping out of savings worldwide.

- The governments of the world facing a liquidity crisis start increasing the money supply progressively higher and higher. Inflation picks up, but when it becomes obvious that the intent is to monetize and devalue all debt, there is a run-out of all paper. Result? Hyperinflationary followed by a deep depression.

These scenarios—and more—are all out there and being debated daily. Are you prepared for another major fall in real estate prices? What if the dollar soars instead of falls and we have better growth than expected and the stock market rallies and the price of gold is cut in half? What if you sell your house just as rents and house prices soar? You want frightening scenarios? I have plenty of them!

There are all kinds of possibilities to keep us up at night. Hopefully you have found the information in this book educational. Hopefully it has stimulated thoughts that you may never have considered. With knowledge comes a certain peace of mind. And in times like these, peace of mind is a rare and precious commodity.

How to Own Gold

Whatever the future brings, the one thing you can count on is an ounce of gold will be an ounce of gold and will, over time, trade for other precious things. Owning gold is the first move toward financial security.

Your first purchase of gold should be to purchase gold coins and/or silver coins. The reason you want to own gold is to have an identifiable medium of exchange recognizable by most individuals in case paper money is no longer acceptable. After all, paper notes are only a promise. Gold or silver coins that you physically own are not a promise—they are tangible commodities and will always be worth something. They might be worth very little and they might be worth a fortune. But they will always have value relative to other values.

Silver dollars are always recognizable and acceptable. Gold coins and bars are a less cumbersome way to store larger sums of wealth. All can be had at a local coin store, but with the Internet today, I'd check the prices at Kitco.com and usagold.com first and compare.

Gold is an insurance policy against those scenarios I just mentioned that keep you up at night. I suggest you have a minimum of 10 percent of your assets in gold and silver coins of all denominations. Twenty or 30 percent is not too much; it depends on your threshold of fear and greed and your particular stage of life. Keep some in your home and the rest in a safety deposit box. I would add cash to that stash also. Try to have enough physical cash of all denominations to get by for a while. Hopefully, you never need to use this insurance policy. But if you do, you will be among the few who will not have to start your wealth accumulation over again.

Having that protection, you might want to invest in precious metals or resource companies. Your options are gold or silver ETFs which you cannot take possession of but, like physical gold, you will profit or lose as the metals go higher or lower. As mentioned above, you can leverage these by buying ETFs or inverse ETFs if you want to hedge your position by going outright short.

Believe me, you will thank your lucky stars if you are heavily invested in physical gold and the U.S. government, or other major governments, announce that they will start selling their gold. The leveraged inverse gold ETF will save you a fortune. I suggest stops on all ETFs, but due to market volatility you may get shaken out. These ETFs are new vehicles, and as of this writing we have not seen a panic in or out of them. How they will react is yet to be determined, so caution is warranted.

My personal favorite investment these days is to accumulate resource exploration companies. Resources are becoming scarcer as demand increases with population and world growth. Gold, silver, and copper will be in high demand for years to come. One good pick of a resource stock that goes from exploring to producing can yield you 10 to 20 times your original investment. These penny stocks are speculative. I have stayed mostly with Canadian and American mines, since there are fewer political risks involved. Some are thinly traded. Just don't forget that on the other side of that potentially precious coin is the possibility that you can lose everything.

Chapter 13

My Final Word on Gold

A s I put this book to bed, I have a little house cleaning to do. There are several recent issues that have been raised, given the renewed interest in gold. The first is a call for a return to the fixed exchange system of Bretton Woods.

On Bretton Woods II

There has been talk of returning to a Bretton Woods–type monetary system. Some call it returning to the gold standard. If you understood anything from this book you understand that Bretton Woods was about as far from a gold standard as you can get. It failed miserably because of it. Any attempt to return to it will fail again.

The gold standard was abandoned in 1913 when the Federal Reserve System was created to replace it. That is when we went off gold, not 1971. 1913 was the beginning of our present day fiat system. The gold standard as we knew it was dead but not buried. That occurred when gold was made illegal and confiscated in 1933. In 1944, when the nations of the world convened to establish the Bretton Woods system, Americans were still legally prohibited from owning gold. *You cannot have a gold standard while prohibiting the use of gold as money!* Bretton Woods was a system where governments could convert their surplus dollars into gold but Americans could not. A return to this kind of a system is not returning to the gold standard.

Worse, it established rules that allowed our competitors to devalue their currencies against the dollar up to 10 percent, if they ran chronic surpluses. Since most nations want to run surpluses by limiting imports and subsidizing exports, they ended up with huge trade surpluses. This led to inflation in their countries, which made their goods more expensive and, therefore, less desirable. They then devalued their currencies again and again to keep their goods cheap. The result was hundreds of devaluations over the years of the Bretton Woods system.

Is this really the monetary system we want to reestablish? The Bretton Woods system was more a system of controlled chaos than stability. It was a system of institutionalized protectionism.

First you would have chronic surpluses build up. Then you had "hot money" flights of capital out of some nations and into others as speculators attacked nation's currencies. Then you would have vehement denials by the government that they would ever devalue their currency. And finally, you would have the inevitable mid-night devaluation, usually just before a weekend. Governments would then blame speculators for causing them to devalue, and the whole process would begin over again.

No, Bretton Woods was not a gold standard. To revisit it would result in the same farce of the past, and gold would end up getting the blame once again. If we are to establish a gold standard we need to look toward the operating rules of the classical gold standard of the nineteenth century, which endured throughout the years.

It is interesting that the call for a return to Bretton Woods is coming from, among others, the IMF. The IMF may be positioning itself for a major move to control monetary policy worldwide. Which brings us to our next issue.

The New SDR Threat

Late on a Friday in August 2009, when most people around the world were not looking, the international monetary system, in an unprecedented move, evolved. We were notified by the IMF of the following:

> Aug. 28 (Bloomberg)—The International Monetary Fund said it today pumped about $250 billion into foreign-exchange reserves worldwide, acting on an April call from leaders of the Group of 20 nations to boost global liquidity.

What this means is that for the first time in history we have a world central bank capable of creating money out of thin air. No longer does the IMF need to borrow money with a vote of all members plus the consent of the U.S. Congress. It can simply create whatever amount of money it needs through the creation of SDRs. Not for itself, mind you, but for the world. The SDR has been around since 1967, but never as a convertible asset.

That changed Friday, August 28th, 2009. The SDR has quietly mutated.

The decision was made in an IMF vote on August 7th. According to the IMF, global reserves will increase from just 33 billion dollars to 283 billion or about 4 percent of global reserves, excluding gold. In addition, the IMF will start issuing SDR notes later this year (China, Brazil, and Russia will be the main buyers). These SDR notes can be counted as part of currency reserves and hence SDR assets could reach 5 percent of total reserve assets later in 2009 and possibly surpass England, Japan, and China in importance as reserve assets. This is a foot in the door.

The prospect of this happening was covered in my article, "The Making of an International Monetary Crisis" (April, 1973):

> The spectacle of billions of inconvertible dollars frozen in the vaults of central banks has brought on cries of condemnation over the dollar's credibility as a reserve currency. The policy makers' theory of a stable yet artificially ever-expanding reserve currency has failed. The solution to the problem (if the policy maker remains consistent) will be to evolve the international monetary system from a system in which an ever-expanding reserve currency provided the world with credit and liquidity, to a system in which an ever-expanding reserve asset will fill that role. Like the dollar, this reserve asset will amount to circulating debt, that is, something owed rather than something owned. It will be a nonmarket instrument, deriving its acceptability from government cooperation and decree, "immune from the laws of the free market and outside the reach of greedy speculators."

Where will this asset come from? Under the Bretton Woods system, dollar reserves were furnished by the U.S. central bank. Both the bank and the asset failed to provide sufficient stability. The next step is to create a world bank (a larger bank of last resort) controlled by an international organization (the IMF) with the power to create a new asset, independent of any single government's monetary policy.

As a supplement to gold and like the dollar before it, this asset should be a credit instrument. Unlike the dollar, it would have the backing of an entire world of central banks. The asset should be ever expanding and should provide both liquidity and stability.

That asset is the SDR and the potential is now a reality. With this unprecedented move, the world is $250 billion "richer." No products were produced. No taxes were raised. Not even one cent was borrowed. The IMF simply created a bookkeeping entry on behalf of those countries it felt worthy of receiving additional reserves. The reserves, SDRs, are a claim to hard currency. The hard currency will be provided by those with "sufficiently strong external positions," in other words, surplus nations.

There is no reason for surplus nations to part with hard currency, save two, that I can think of: altruism or power. And in my opinion they are having a go at the latter. My read on this is that the surplus nations have just made an end run around the United States and the U.S. Congress who have veto power over IMF decisions. Surplus nations can now provide voluntary trading arrangements with nonsurplus (importing) nations with the IMF as broker. This sounds like a mechanism for the surplus nations to provide buying power to importing nations at the expense of us all.

The ability to inflate has now been augmented. It has transcended national boundaries from national central banks to a world central bank. This new bank now has the power to create money. Inflation is no longer limited to one currency but will affect all paper currencies in the world. We now have the prospect of synchronized international inflation. It's not enough that citizens throughout the world had to keep a keen eye on their nation's central bank; now we all need to keep an eye on the IMF.

The IMF's Board of Governors, a group never elected to office, unknown to most, and accountable to no one, has now gained the power to create new claims on production without legal limits or oversight from any regulatory body. All it need do is vote for more SDRs.

Given the announcement-in-the-dead-of-night tactics just employed, I suggest we all sharpen our eyesight. This development doesn't change the inflation outlook for the next month or even for the next year. But make no mistake—the so-called "powers that be" just took the fiat system and the inflation threat to a new level.

(Update: As this book goes to print, an informal proposal has been offered that the IMF be allowed to create two trillion dollars more in SDRs.)

On QE2

There is in any and all monetary systems, quantitative easing (QE). Under the gold standard money increases due to the production of gold by miners. Under today's fiat standard money increases by the decree of a 12-member board called the Federal Reserve

Board. Under an ideal fiat standard the money supply would be fixed at a low and stable rate of about 3 to 5 percent and not tampered with. But under any monetary system, the money supply would increase over time.

For this reason the entire concept of quantitative easing makes little sense. The only question is not whether money should increase but rather how and by how much. There are some commentators that have recently advocated ending quantitative easing. They equate it with inflation. They actually are advocating a zero increase in money supply to prevent inflation. Needless to say this monetary policy if implemented would send the country, if not the world, into a deflationary depression. This underlines the point that a little bit of knowledge is a dangerous thing. Quantitative easing is the norm under the gold standard or the fiat standard, not the exception.

There is nothing wrong with quantitative easing per se. It is the natural state of events. I have been arguing that we should move toward a monetary system where the quantity of money and its price (interest rates) should be determined by the free market. Others prefer that this be left to the arbitrary decision of bureaucrats. In either case the money supply will increase. There can be no such thing as QE, QE1, or QE2. These are moot points.

Those who are concerned about the Fed's increase of the money supply are really concerned that the Fed is depreciating the dollar. My views on this subject were laid out in Chapter 3, "Why Prices Are Not Skyrocketing." But I think the essential point here is that the Fed's injection of funds into the banking system (QE1) was an act of a bank of last resort bolstering the system's capital in order to prevent insolvency and systemic damage. It was not the act of a monetary authority that wants to create inflation.

The Fed has the power to decrease the money supply as fast as it increased it, if necessary. My main concern is not that the Fed will allow inflation to progressively increase. I do not believe this Fed has either the desire or the power to allow that to happen.

First, the Fed has nothing to gain, and everything to lose if it allows inflation to progressively rise. It will face the same anger of the populace as is being witnessed in other countries around the world that attempted such policies. And second, progressive inflation will lead to negative consequences far faster than any benefit of inflation could yield. And third, everyone is looking for inflation. There is no way the Fed can pull off a hidden inflation. A million voices will be heard in protest as soon as prices begin to rise progressively.

My concern is more that the Fed's erratic stop-and-go monetary tactics are disruptive and can create unforeseen consequences; it has the potential of undermining confidence in the monetary unit that could lead to a sudden breakdown of the dollar as a prime currency. The threat and possibility of a total rejection of the fiat system and the subsequent breakdown of the monetary system, resulting in an immediate hyperinflation, is a higher possibility than any possibility of a prolonged progressive inflation.

This is why I argue that the money supply should be set at a low and stable rate, and interest rates be allowed to seek their market level. At any time, the Fed can employ its mandate of bank of last resort and backstop the system should this become necessary. But this is the exception to the normal operations of the Fed. It is an option used only in rare times of huge stress and rarely need be taken.

The entire concept of a Federal Reserve System to replace the gold standard was flawed from the beginning. But it is all we have at the present moment, and we need to use it in the most rational way we can. The direction we need to be moving in is toward greater capital requirements and less leverage in the present banking system. Which leads us to this next and final bit of housekeeping.

The Banking System of a Free Society

There is a continuing debate within the Austrian School of Economics and among other free market advocates already looking toward the establishment of a free society and a return to the gold standard. It is whether the banking system should, under a gold standard, by law, be forced to print only those paper claims to gold that it has on deposit in gold at any one time. In other words, should we as a nation be on a 100 percent reserve standard? Or should we be on a fractional reserve system where leverage can be used?

The argument for a 100 percent reserve standard is persuasive. If we ever return to a gold standard, it is argued, any leveraging of gold would amount to fraud, since a bank cannot truly guarantee it can convert its outstanding claims to gold even though it promises to do so. Hence, fractional reserve banking is both fraudulent and reckless. This is what leads to bank runs, bank failures, panics, and monetary as well as economic crises.

The counterargument is that since people rarely all want to convert their dollars to gold at the same time, it is not unreasonable for a bank to leverage its gold. In this way it can provide more credit to society, and economic activity and production will be enhanced. Prudent lending is what is needed, not the restrictive hand of government.

Interesting argument, isn't it? One argues on moral grounds, the other on practical grounds. I have always held there should be no dichotomy between the moral and the practical, and I think this argument can be resolved to both camps' satisfaction.

Why must there be a choice? Why must it be either/or? Why can't both exist side by side? In a free society, we allow choice. We also allow risk taking. This is what free enterprise is all about. If a consumer wants the safest form of savings he should be allowed to deposit his money in a storehouse or a bank that insures and guarantees his money on demand. He will probably be charged a fee for this service.

But he should also have the choice to place his money in a savings account where the banker will be allowed to lend it out. For this he should be entitled to a small return on his money. Some loans may be longer than other loans, so there should be an agreement established between depositor and banker that those funds lent out for longer periods of time cannot be called on demand. In other words a "time deposit" requires notice. That gives the banker time to convert funds lent out into funds on hand.

So, in a free society there is no reason why many different kinds of banks issuing various kinds of products can't coexist. The point is there should be no such thing as a banking system. Just as we have no steel system or lumber system, there should be no banking system.

In a free enterprise society, there should be competing companies within a competitive industry. The stock market offers an excellent example. We have the choice of investing in common stock or preferred stock. We have the choice of buying on margin, buying options, or leveraged ETFs. We can buy futures contracts to hedge, or lock in a price, or short a position. Or we can choose not to invest at all.

If we do choose to invest, we accept the risks. No one invests with the idea that he or she will lose their investment, but we all know it is possible. Holding your money in cash is safe, but not an investment. Giving your money to a bank to lend out for an interest rate return is.

As long as the terms of banking and note issuance are explicit and no fraud exists, there is no reason why those that want a high degree of protection of their wealth cannot secure it and those who want to invest or speculate in order to obtain a higher rate of return on their money should not be allowed to.

In the last analysis, individuals will look to place their excess funds with companies of the highest reputation and best track record. They will look for accounts that are insured and choose to store wealth or invest wealth as they see fit. Whether stocks, bonds, banks, or brokerages, people have a choice—and none of these choices provides absolute certainty.

In Conclusion

So, I will say at the end what I said at the beginning of this journey: there is no Utopia—not in economies, not in politics, and not in investing. Gold is what it is: a rare and precious metal with particular qualities that make it an effective medium of exchange. And today, it happens to be a good investment vehicle. There is no guarantee that gold will go up or down in the future. That will be determined by the market. There is no guarantee that a gold standard will prevent future panics or crises. It will not. But the closer we come to one the greater will be the security of money, hence the stability of the economy.

There may come a day when individuals everywhere decide that their money is just too important to be left in the hands of government. When that day occurs, it will be the beginning of a freer, more predictable, and more stable society.

But just as a democratic, constitutional republic as we have here in America is, at best, the least-worse system of government, and free market capitalism is, for all its drawbacks, the best path to prosperity, so gold is the best money and the gold standard the best monetary system known to mankind thus far. Interestingly, all are interdependent. You cannot have a gold standard without free market capitalism, free international trade, and the objective laws that protect individual and property rights; this can only be achieved with fiscal discipline and a limited government. As I said before: if we are ever going to return to a gold standard it will be on the wings of capitalism—and not before.

It is to this end, and for these conditions, that I will continue to fight. If you are interested in participating in this intellectual battle, I invite you to join me at my website.

For more articles on gold, weekly commentary, market updates on stocks and gold, investing strategies, visit Paulnathan.biz.

Recommended Reading

The first book I ever read on economics was *Economics in One Lesson* by Henry Hazlitt. Thereafter, I read everything by him I could get my hands on. Henry Hazlitt makes economics fun. *Economics in One Lesson* made reading economics not only fun but interesting, simple, and clear. One of the next books I read that caused me to fall in love with the subject was his fictional book, *Time Will Run Back*. It is a marvelous book of a young man that finds himself in the position of dictator of a command economy. It is a book about the rediscovery of capitalism.

Milton Friedman also made economics fun, interesting, and clear. His books *Dollars and Deficits* and *Capitalism and Freedom* are two that influenced me profoundly. Still, his *A Monetary History of the United States, 1867–1960*, which he co-wrote with Anna Schwartz, helped win him a Nobel Prize and brought him recognition as a scholar. No one influenced economics more than Milton Friedman in the 1960s and 1970s, and it was to his great credit that he achieved acclaim academically as well as from the average American citizen.

Ludwig von Mises, the father of Austrian Economics, is my intellectual mentor. When it comes to the nuts and bolts of economics, von Mises is the source. His book, *The Theory of Money and Credit*, and his treatise, *Human Action*, provide the theoretical ammunition that allows us to understand the workings of an economy and the how and why of it. It is not fun reading, but it is indispensible to anyone wanting a real education in economics.

Murray Rothbard wrote a wonderful little book called *What Has Government Done to Our Money?*, which makes the case for a 100 percent reserve banking system. While I disagree with its objective, his clear and concise reasoning together with his description of the abuses of fractional reserve banking make it must reading. He is known for his dissection of America's Great Depression, from the book of the same name. It is perhaps the best analysis of the causes and lack of cures of that period.

In the field of investment books, two stand out that shaped my investment philosophy. The first is *The Death of the Dollar* by William F. Rickenbacker, and *How You Can Profit from the Coming Devaluation* by Harry Browne. Both are instructive in the ways of the world, and both pose scenarios that are watched closely to this day. They were among the first books to alert people to the threat of dollar depreciation—and how to protect oneself through the ownership of gold, gold stocks, and diversification.

And finally, the works of Ayn Rand. Before I found economics, I found Ayn. I have to thank her and her recommended reading list for where I am today. Ayn Rand inspired millions and changed their lives through her novels, *The Fountainhead* and *Atlas Shrugged*. But it was her academic works that provide the philosophy necessary to recognize and understand Statism when you see it and provide the tools to fight it and win. Ayn Rand's philosophy is a profoundly personal thing. It was presented by her as a philosophy, not to propagate, but to live. I highly recommend all of her books to those who enjoy the power of ideas.

Bibliography

Browne, Harry. *How You Can Profit from the Coming Devaluation*, New Rochelle, NY: Arlington House, 1970.

CNN.com. "Zimbabwe Inflation Hits 11,200,000." Retrieved 08-19-2008 from http://edition.cnn.com/2008/BUSINESS/08/19/zimbabwe.inflation/index.html.

Fisher, Irving. *The Purchasing Power of Money: Its Determination and Relation to Credit, Interest and Crises*. New York: Macmillan Company, 1912.

Friedman, Milton. *Capitalism and Freedom*. Chicago: The University of Chicago Press, 1962.

———. *Dollars and Deficits: Living with America's Economic Problems*. Englewood Cliffs, NJ: Prentice Hall, 1968.

Friedman, Milton, and Anna Schwartz. *A Monetary History of the United States, 1867–1960*. Princeton, NJ: Princeton University Press, 1963.

Hazlitt, Henry. *Economics in One Lesson*. New York: Three Rivers Press, 1979.

———. *Time Will Run Back*. New Rochelle, NY: Arlington House, 1966.

———. *What You Should Know About Inflation*. Princeton, NJ: D. Van Nostrand Company, 1960.

Rand, Ayn. *Atlas Shrugged*. New York: Random House, 1957.

———. *The Fountainhead*. Indianapolis, IN: Bobbs-Merrill, 1943.

———. *Capitalism: The Unknown Ideal*. New York: New American Library, 1966.

Rothbard, Murray. *America's Great Depression*, 5th ed. Auburn, AL: Ludwig von Mises Institute, 2000.

———. *What Has Government Done to Our Money?* Auburn, AL: Ludwig von Mises Institute, 1963.

von Mises, Ludwig. *Human Action: A Treatise on Economics*. New Haven, CT: Yale University Press, 1949.

———. *The Theory of Money and Credit*. London, UK: Jonathan Cape, 1938.

Rastello, Sandrine. "IMF Pumps $250 Billion into Global Foreign-Currency Reserves," *Bloomberg,* 8/28/09. Retrieved from: www.bloomberg .com/apps/news?pid=newsarchive&sid=a_7xC2NrTkkU.

Rickenbacker, William F. *Death of the Dollar: How the Money Managers Are Savaging Your Dollar—And What You Must Do to Protect Yourself in the Coming Collapse*. New Rochelle, NY: Arlington House, 1968.

About the Author

The first time I ever saw a gold coin was in 1968. I had seen lots of silver dollars but gold was illegal to own and I had never actually seen a gold coin. I was standing in the elevator of the Empire State Building, descending to the ground floor, and I noticed a gold coin hanging around the neck of the gentleman next to me. It was hanging as a medallion over his cream-colored turtleneck sweater. I was so focused on its beauty, I barely noticed the woman by his side. It was Ayn Rand and the man wearing the gold coin was her husband, Frank O'Connor.

I had come to the Empire State Building to attend a lecture that evening by Ayn Rand on the state of the nation. Ayn had an institute in the building that provided lectures on all sorts of subjects—from economics to politics, philosophy, psychology, and much more. It was there that I first became interested in economics and gold.

I signed up for a 10-lecture course on "The Economics of a Free Society," given by an unknown named Alan Greenspan. (To this day, I am one of the few who can speak Greenspanese fluently.) In the lecture series he often referenced the gold standard. That sparked my interest in gold and the gold standard, then gold stocks, and finally gold trading. However, it was that first glimpse of the gold coin hanging around Frank O'Connor's neck that led me to where I am today.

I met and spoke with Ayn, and she gave me a list of that year's classes and lectures. As she looked at me I couldn't help notice her eyes: They were probing, intelligent, and benevolent all at the same time. They were huge. Never before, or since, have I ever felt so *perceived*. I had the pleasure of going to many lectures Ayn gave over the next year. Little did I know then that her book *Atlas Shrugged* would become the second best-selling book of all time, second only to the Bible. Currently, her books are enjoying a major comeback with a brand new audience. I do believe Ayn Rand is more popular today than she was when she was alive.

At Ayn Rand's institute, the Foundation for the New Intellectual, they also had a bookstore. Among the books recommended was *Economics in One Lesson* by Henry Hazlitt. That one little book caused me to fall in love with economics. For me it turned "the dismal science" into a fascinating journey. I later made contact with Hazlitt, and he became instrumental in helping me establish myself as a writer. To this day I try to emulate his clarity and his simplicity.

In Greenspan's lecture series he constantly referenced the nineteenth-century gold standard. Already having a curiosity about gold, I started researching it and found very little information about what a gold standard was and its evolution. That remains true to this day. Greenspan was instrumental in forming my economic viewpoint and focusing my attention on the importance of gold in a monetary system.

By 1971 I had accumulated enough knowledge on economics that I was writing a column in a small-town paper called "Dollars and Sense." (I think I could have been the first one to use that title.) By that time, I had read the *Theory of Money and Credit* and *Human Action* by Ludwig von Mises, most of the classical works of the great masters, and was deeply engrossed in *A Monetary History of the United States, 1867–1960* by Milton Friedman.

I was taking Economics 101 in college but in my boredom with the class, I saw an opportunity to take an undergraduate course in international economics as an exchange student in London that summer. I bluffed my way into two different college professor's offices asking for sponsorship. I was turned down by the first but remarkably accepted by the second. I wasn't interested in a grade—I'm not even sure to this day whether I was legally supposed to take the class having just begun college—I was only interested in getting to London and studying economics from that vantage point.

Three months later I found myself in London enrolled in a bunch of unimportant classes. However, I made an agreement to send one paper on current events every week for 10 weeks to the professor on international economics that I signed up with. I spent the 10 weeks at the London School of Economics Library reading every interesting book I could get my hands on. A monetary crisis was brewing that year, gold was soaring, and I was viewing it from abroad.

Somewhere along the line I stopped getting comments from my economics professor back home. I thought the papers I was sending were pretty good and right up to the minute—applying theory to current-day economic and monetary affairs. When I returned home I had to hunt the guy down. He wouldn't see me for several days. Finally he allowed me a few minutes.

I walked in and he looked a little flustered. I asked him if he had received the 10 papers I had sent to him. He almost yelled at me, "This is junk!" I asked him, "Why?" He said, "The money supply does not cause inflation!" I told him that Professor Milton Friedman had suggested differently. (Now you have to understand that in 1971, Friedman was regarded as a radical and extremist. He won the Nobel Prize for economics not too many years later, but it was only after totally refuting present-day established economic theory.) The professor said Friedman's theories were simplistic and that monetary theory was more complicated than that. Anyway, he refused to pass me.

Undaunted, I worked up a couple of articles based on those papers the economics professor had turned down. I sent them to Henry Hazlitt. He liked them and suggested I send them to *Barron's*. Robert Bleiberg, the editor, said he would recommend me to *The Freeman*, a magazine about liberty. Hazlitt also said he would forward them to Leonard Read, of the Foundation for Economic Education. The magazine and the foundation were connected. Two weeks later I received a letter from the editor of *The Freeman*, Paul Piorot. He complimented me on the articles and called them "the most lucid account of the international monetary muddle I've seen." They published my articles, and they wound up in many libraries here and around the globe. The last thing he asked was, "By the way, who is Paul Stevens?" Paul Stevens was my pen name at that time. I had come out of nowhere.

In 1972 I became adviser to my mother, Tonie Nathan, who was the vice presidential candidate on the first ticket of the

Libertarian Party, with John Hospers. Tonie Nathan became the first woman in history to receive an electoral vote for vice president. We toured and made many appearances; Tonie was an excellent spokesperson for the ideas espoused by the Libertarian Party.

I wrote several other articles on gold for *The Freeman* in the early 1970s. I was among a handful who fought for the legalization of gold, which finally occurred in 1975. That year I was invited to attend a seminar on "The Monetary Problems of Our Times." It was a tribute to Ludwig von Mises, sponsored by the Liberty Fund. There were about a dozen of us invited: Henry Hazlitt; author/professor Hans Sennholz; author and professor Benjamin Rogge, Dean of Economics and author of many textbooks on economics; Phillip Crane, Congressman and co-author with Ron Paul of legislation to legalize gold in the United States; William Peterson of the Department of Commerce; John Exter, Central Banker; and many more.

All those in attendance were in their sixties and above. One Paul Nathan, 29, unknown, bearded, and dressed in a sport coat and turtleneck shirt rather than a suit and tie was rather conspicuous in his unconventionality. But then, so was my past.

I do not consider myself a Republican, a conservative, a gold bug, or a libertarian. I voted for Reagan in 1980, and I voted for Clinton in his second term. I believe that economics is neither liberal nor conservative, just as I believe that science is neither liberal nor conservative.

I have been a full-time investor since 1968. My first investment was in Homestake Mines. I lived through the closing of the gold window, the great inflation of the 1970s, gas lines, and the imposition of wage and price controls during the 1970s; the Hunt Brothers' attempt to corner the silver market; the Reagan Revolution; and the birth of the bull market in stocks in 1982.

In August of 1982, as an investment adviser, I sent out an alert to sell gold and buy common stocks as gold was near its highs and the Dow was trading near its lows. I projected that the biggest common stock bull market of our lifetime was ahead of us, suggesting the Dow would triple by the end of the decade. I coined the phrase "technological revolution" and compared what was to come to the industrial revolution.

I became a full-time private investor in 2000 and recommended once again accumulating gold and gold stocks at $250 an ounce. In the last decade I have made a profit 9 years out of 10, culminating with a 40 percent and 80 percent profit in 2008 and 2009, during which it is estimated that 95 percent of investors lost money. I called the top of the market in July 2007 and suggested going short. And I bought stocks in March 2009 at the market lows.

In 2010 I began my commentary and investment website, Paulnathan.biz. And in 2011, I published a book.

Now comes the fun part—the future.

Index

Index